Nonnie Talks about Mental Health

Suggested for children in grades 3-8 and their trusted adults

By Dr. Mary Jo Podgurski
Consultants Rueben Brock, PhD, LPC
Bob Selverstone, PhD
Illustrations by Alice M. Burroughs

An Interactive Book for Children and Adults

NONNIE TALKS ABOUT MENTAL HEALTH: VOLUME TWELVE OF THE NONNIE SERIES

Copyright ©2021 by Dr. Mary Jo Podgurski
All rights reserved

No part of this book may be reproduced in any manner whatsoever without written permission from the author. For information, write AcademyPress, 410 N. Main Street, Washington, PA 15301. The AcacemyPress is the publishing arm of the Academy for Adolescent Health, Inc.

The Academy for Adolescent Health, Inc. website is http://healthyteens.com/

Illustrations created by Alice M. Burroughs are the property of the Academy for Adolescent Health, Inc., and are copyright protected. All rights reserved.

Photographs were purchased for use in this book or were donated and used with permission, for exclusive use in this book.

ISBN: 978-1-7343001-3-0

Dedication

This one is dedicated with all my love to the young people I serve.

Thank you to my generous, wise reviewers:
Karen Bennett
LaShauna Carruthers
Dale and Darlene Emme
Joan Garrity
Dr. Tracie Q. Gilbert
Shea Hatfield
Dr. Monique Howard
Joseph Mahoney, LSW
Rodney Maze, RN
Joni Schwager, LSW
Bill Taverner, MEd

Introduction: Thoughts about a Child's Developmental Readiness for the Nonnie Series:

Many people ask me for help in determining a child's readiness for the books in the Nonnie Series.

Children today can glean information from online sources in a mouse click or smartphone search, but they are not always as comfortable sharing their concerns with adults. Adults, conversely, may not know how to address complicated topics, or may think a child is "too young" or unaware. I think the power of the Nonnie Series™ is the message "It's OK to talk about this together" – for adults and children!

Monitor your children's ability to process information. Maturity and age are often unrelated to reading ability; an adult can read and explain complicated words and concepts, but a child's curiosity and eagerness to embrace knowledge are important considerations. Adults need to "articulate the obvious" when educating children. It's important to empower. Too often adults think the word empower means they give power to young people; the opposite is true. When we empower young people, we guide them to find their own power.

Try paraphrasing this message: "I'd like to look at this book with you. I think you may be interested in the topic. We can read the book at your own pace. You can talk with me about anything and I will respect you. I will always respect your feelings."

I suggest grade levels as opposed to age because I'm sensitive to reading ability, but I truly do not feel the books should be limited to one group. For example, not all third- or fourth-graders will be developmentally ready for all the chapters in the books; the books should be read at a child's speed. On the other hand, not all seventh- or eighth-graders will be interested in interacting with an adult to address these topics, but some will enjoy learning and communicating with someone they trust.

No one is more important to a child than a trusted adult. Learning takes place when we process information; communicate with the young people in your life and share your values with respect.

Each child is different. Let your children lead you. Their interest, more than their grade level or age, should be your guide.

Thank you for listening and caring about young people.

With respect and admiration,

Mary Jo Podgurski

Dr. Mary Jo Podgurski

About Consultant Author Rueben Brock

DR. RUEBEN BROCK is an assistant professor of psychology at California University of Pennsylvania. With a PhD in counseling psychology, Brock focuses on clinical issues in mental health and drug and alcohol treatment.

He currently serves as president of board of directors for the American Psychological Association's Minority Fellowship Program.

He is a licensed counselor in private practice.

Dr. Brock is also a jazz musician and filmmaker. His newest film, Discovering Autism is available on YouTube.

About Consultant Author Bob Selverstone

BOB SELVERSTONE, Ph.D. has been a licensed psychologist in private practice in Westport, CT, for 40 years – overlapping his 35 years as a public school counselor, Director of his school district's Human Relations Program and high school and graduate school teacher of courses in Values Clarification and Human Sexuality.

He has written for numerous professional journals, been featured in a dozen award-winning educational videos, and has appeared on many radio and TV programs. His PBS/Children's Television Workshop special, "*What Kids Want to Know About Sex and Growing Up,*" was nominated for an Emmy in 1992.

He has conducted over 1000 workshops and presentations to professional and parent groups on issues of social and emotional health, values, communication, self-esteem, relationships and sexuality.

He presented invited testimony before two Congressional Committees and is a recipient of the CT Education Association's *Human Relations Award*.

How to use this book:

Nonnie Talks about Mental Health was created to be used by children and adults together. Please read this book with someone who matters to you.

For Children:

This picture means you may color the page if you wish. This symbol * or a red word means a word may be new. The Glossary on pages 84–90 will help with new words. Words written in blue are especially important messages or are for you, the reader. Groups of words marked with a blue asterisk above the words (like *) refer to a footnote (a sentence at the bottom of the page) to explain something in more detail.

A What do YOU think? page is a great page to help people talk with each other.
Please talk with a trusted adult!
Please listen!

Most important:
Every person is different.
Each child who picks up this book is different.
Each adult who reads this book with a child is different.
Some ideas may be easy to understand. That's OK.
Some ideas may be difficult to understand. That's OK.

©2021 ~ All rights reserved   AcademyPress ~ http://www.healthyteens.com/

How to use this book:
For Parents, Teachers and Trusted Adults:

1. I strongly recommend reading the book without your child first. Consider any concerns you may have with the material and prepare for your child's possible questions.
2. The book is divided into chapters. The chapters are only suggestions; they divide the content to allow for pleasant learning. The book may be read as one part, two parts, three parts, four parts—it's up to you. You know your children best. Please monitor their attention, their interest, and their awareness and understanding of the concepts.
3. The topic of mental health is a critical issue in today's world. Teaching acceptance for difference and empathy for another's life experiences are key to developing a positive person. Mental health stigma is common. You are your child's first teacher. Communicate and be an empathic role model!
4. As Nonnie, Tamika and Alex discuss, mental health is as important as physical health, but is often misunderstood. We seldom chide people with a physical injury for not "shaking it off" or making themselves better. Mental illness, in my opinion, should be viewed with the same compassion as physical illness. I was diagnosed with breast cancer in 2019. No one suggested I could recover from surgery without support. I was seen. Yet, the young people I serve with a diagnosis of clinical depression or bipolar are often ignored. No one should be invisible.
5. Just as children's physical and emotional development are unique, so is their readiness for information. Please let the children you love be your guides.
6. The What do YOU Think? pages should be completed at a child's pace, but are important. Learning takes place when we process information.
7. The Appendices on pages 72—83 include original artwork, personal thoughts from a young person and a parent who've "been there" and other resources.

Most important:
Be aware of the "music" (tone of voice) behind your words. Adult modeling and acceptance of skills like respect and empathy are vital.

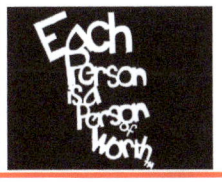

Please teach children the importance of respect.

Mary Jo Podgurski

©2021 ~ All rights reserved

AcademyPress ~ http://www.healthyteens.com/

Nonnie Talks about Mental Health

Suggested for children in grades 3-8 and their trusted adults

By Dr. Mary Jo Podgurski
Consultants Rueben Brock, PhD, LPC
Bob Selverstone, PhD
Illustrations by Alice M. Burroughs

An Interactive Book for Children and Adults

©2021, Mary Jo Podgurski, RNC, EdD
Academy for Adolescent Health, Inc.
410 N. Main Street
Washington, PA 15301
1 (888) 301 2311
podmj@healthyteens.com
http://www.healthyteens.com/

Chapter One: The Story Begins

Did you ever have a huge question?

Most children wonder about a lot of different things.

Would you like to read a story about two children with lots of questions? The story may answer some of your questions.

If you still have questions when the story is finished, please ask your parents or a trusted adult.

Once upon a time….

Alex and Tamika are best friends.

They can't remember a time when they weren't friends.

Their parents said they were even in the same play group when they were only two years old! As they grow older, their friendship also changes and grows.

Alex and Tamika are very curious. When something confuses them or makes them wonder, they often turn to the trusted adults in their families for answers.

They speak with their parents, Tamika's older brother, their aunts and uncles, and their teachers and other trusted adults*.

A trusted adult is someone who respects young people, listens to their thoughts, and keeps promises.

Alex's grandma is a nurse and a teacher and a counselor.

Tamika and he call her Nonnie. When they're confused or curious about something they often talk with Nonnie.
She listens to them, hears them, respects them, and helps them grow and learn.

Nonnie is a trusted adult.

 Have you ever wanted to talk with a trusted adult? Who are the trusted adults in your life?

Alex and Tamika are ending 7th grade.

Friendships are very important to them now.

They care about what their friends think about them.

They spend a lot of time thinking about how they dress for school and activities. They text and talk on the phone a lot!

Because Tamika and Alex liked teaching their peers* they completed formal training as peer educators*. As peer educators, their own self-worth* grows.

Peer educators teach and model healthy choices to other young people. Nonnie says, "When an adult teaches young people, the message is heard as a whisper. When a peer educator teaches, it's heard as a shout."

Every time they teach, they learn.

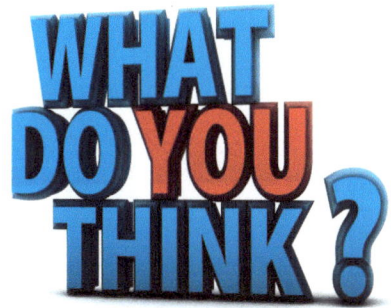

What do YOU Think?

How important are friendships to you?

Do you think you'd like to teach your peers?
Why or why not? Do you like talking in front of others?
What do you think your peers need to hear and learn?
How can you help your peers learn what they need?

Please draw or write your thoughts here:

Chapter Two: Growing and Learning

This semester at school, Tamika and Alex were honored by a membership in the National Junior Honor Society (NJHS)*.

Both their families were very excited. Tamika and Alex stood proudly before the American flag while Nonnie took their picture.

Alex was especially happy to see his cousin, Sara. She enlisted in the military after high school and was home on leave. Alex was thrilled she could attend his JNHS induction. He was close to Sara and carried the pic she sent him on his phone.

Tamika was equally proud. Her Great Uncle Isaac was a retired career officer in the Air Force. He made a special trip to honor her at the NJHS induction. He wore his uniform and saluted Tamika and Alex. Nonnie took a pic!

Tamika and Alex loved having their extended families with them to celebrate. The only person missing was Tamika's older brother, LeBron. He was in his last year of college and finishing his internship*. He could not leave school until spring break.

When LeBron arrived in a few weeks, Alex and Tamika were so happy, they didn't even wait for him to see his fiancé'*. They were at Tamika's house as soon as they left school. LeBron was always so much fun. He could be counted on for entertainment. He knew the best movies to stream and was a video game wiz.

They had so many questions. They couldn't wait to hear about his plans for after college. Would he go to on to law school or get a job? Would he move home? Would he enlist like his Great Uncle Isaac? When, they wanted to ask, was the wedding?

When they saw LeBron, they were shocked!
He was quiet. He did not smile. He wasn't himself at all!

No matter what they did, they could not coax LeBron into joining them.

He wasn't interested in movies or video games.

He wouldn't take a walk with them.

He just shook his head when they asked him to take them for a ride in his car.

He went to his room and skipped dinner.
No one they knew ever skipped a meal!
And his mom made his favorite, mac n cheese!

When Tamika asked her mom what to do, she suggested they go to Alex's house and hang out. They were full of questions.

What was wrong with LeBron? Why did he skip dinner?

Why were they told to go to Alex's house?

Tamika and Alex didn't know Tamika's mom had already called Alex's dad. Nonnie was on her way.

Tamika and Alex also didn't know LeBron left his bedroom and spoke with his mom and dad right after they left the house.

Later, they would understand LeBron wanted to protect them. He didn't know Nonnie would help them understand. They knew talking with his parents was the best thing LeBron could do. They knew they needed to talk with trusted adults too.

LeBron told his parents what happened at school. He met his roommate Josh freshman year. They are best friends.

LeBron came home from a full day of classes and found Josh still in bed. He tried to wake him and could not. There was an empty bottle of pills beside Josh's bed. LeBron called for help.

LeBron was still troubled. He knew Josh was often sad, but never expected him to try to take his own life. He said it is hard to stop thinking about what happened, even though Josh is now okay.

When Tamika and Alex arrived at Nonnie's house, she said, "I'm here. We can sit quietly together, we can play a game, we can take a walk, or I can answer your questions."

Tamika said, "I have lots of questions." She turned to Alex and asked, "Do you?"

Alex shook his head. "Maybe later," he said. "I need to take Max for a walk." He grabbed the leash and his dog and ran out the door.

"But, Alex," Tamika called as he left but he didn't hear her. She snorted. "Why is he acting so weird? Weirder than usual!"

Tamika rolled her eyes, and then sank down on the porch love seat beside Nonnie.

"Nonnie," she said. "I have so many questions. I know mom and dad are trying to help my brother. May I ask you my questions?"

Of course, Nonnie said 'yes' right away. She told Tamika she spoke with her mom and dad on her way to Alex's house.

"You can ask me anything, Tamika," Nonnie said, which was just what Tamika knew she would say.
Tamika hesitated.
Nonnie waited.
Tamika sighed.
Nonnie waited.

Waiting to listen is part of holding space*

Then, Tamika mumbled, "It feels strange asking you questions without Alex. Here's my first question: Why is Alex avoiding what's happening with LeBron?"

Nonnie said, "I'm not sure, but the way he ran out of the house gives me a hint. I think Alex is afraid."

"Of what?" Tamika asked, confused.

"Most people fear something they don't understand," Nonnie said. "What was LeBron's body language* like?" Tamika and Alex learned to watch people's body language to better understand them when Nonnie taught them about disability*.

Tamika got it. She said, "LeBron wouldn't talk with us. Or take us for a ride. Or go on a walk. He even skipped mac n cheese!"
Nonnie nodded. "Did he seem sad?"

Tamika said, "He seemed more than sad. Deep sad. Big sad."

*See *Nonnie Talks about Disability* for more.

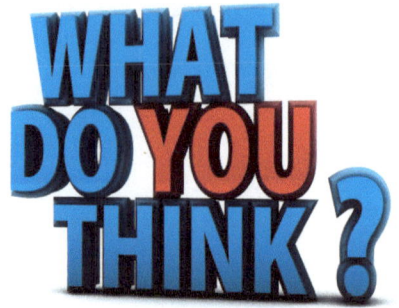

What do YOU Think?

Tamika said her brother is "big sad". What do you think she means?

Have you felt sad? Feeling sad is a normal and common* emotion. What do you think Tamika meant by "big sad"? Do you know anyone who felt very sad? Have you ever felt very sad? Share how being sad feels to you.

Please draw or write your thoughts here:

While Nonnie and Tamika talked about feeling sad, Alex returned. He sat for a minute on the edge of a porch chair and then stood up, mumbled "I'm tired," and went into the house.

Tamika shrugged. "So," she said. "Do you know what happened at LeBron's school? And, why do you think Alex is frightened?"

Nonnie smiled. She loved the way Tamika was direct and open with her questions. She also loved her concern for Alex.

"First things first," Nonnie said. "Do want to know the truth? It may be hard to hear."

Tamika nodded. "I do," she said. "I'm old enough to know."

Nonnie began, "LeBron's college roommate…"
Tamika interrupted, "Josh?"

Josh had spent many holiday breaks with her family, and LeBron had flown to New York to visit Josh's family. Tamika liked him a lot.

When she flew with her mom and Josh to bring her grandparents home, Josh's family opened their home to them and they saved hotel costs. Her grandparent's apartment was too small for all of them. Her grandpa was sick* and Tamika remembered her mom saying Josh's family's hospitality helped.

*See *Nonnie Talks about Death* for the full story.

Chapter Three: Depression

Nonnie remembered and said, "Yes, honey. Josh. He's been very depressed*. He wouldn't go to a counselor*. He took a lot of pills that weren't safe in large amounts. LeBron found him unconscious* in their dorm room."

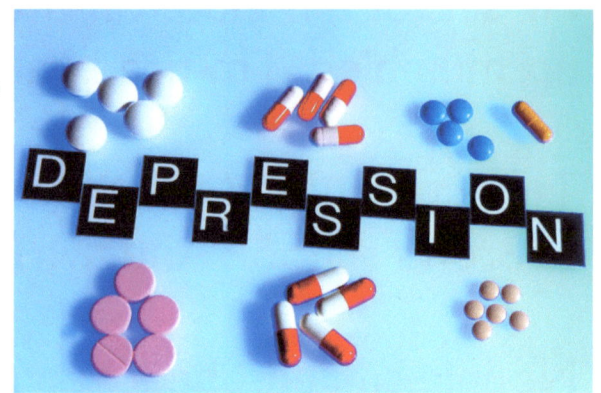

She quickly added, "LeBron made calls to the campus hotline and Josh was taken to the hospital. He's all right now."

Tamika gasped and her eyes filled with tears. "I'm so glad he's okay," she said.

Nonnie opened her arms and Tamika fell into them for a nice, long hug. Tamika closed her eyes, taking slow, deep breaths like Nonnie taught the children. Nonnie gently rubbed her back. Then, she opened her eyes and said, "Now I have more questions!"

Tamika's questions were wise.

She wanted to know what made Josh so sad.
She wanted to know why Josh wouldn't go to counseling*.
She wanted to know why Josh took the pills.
She wanted to know why LeBron was sad, too.
She wanted to know why Alex was avoiding their conversation.
She didn't tell Nonnie she was already worried about Alex…

Nonnie began to answer all her questions honestly.

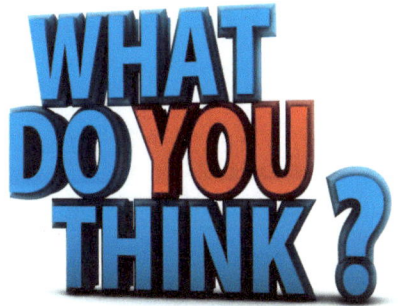

What do YOU Think?

Tamika asks great questions. She's comfortable asking Nonnie.

Would you like answers to Tamika's questions? Have you heard of someone who was very depressed? Do you have a trusted adult to answer your questions? If you cannot think of a trusted adult, please look at pages 26 and 27 for ways to find one.

Please draw or write your thoughts here:

Nonnie said, "I don't know why Josh was sad, but I believe he was clinically depressed*. Many people are sad, and some may even be depressed due to a loss or a temporary sorrow. When the depression doesn't go away or is serious, a person may not feel life is worth living."

Tamika was solemn. "How do you know if someone is clinically depressed, Nonnie?" she asked.

"There are signs of depression, honey. These signs can help us support others. Would you like to talk about the signs with me?"

Tamika brightened. Nonnie knew her very well. "I like to think and talk about things with you, Nonnie." She paused a minute. "Not without Alex. Let me run and get him," she added.

Alex returned with Tamika, but after a minute, he excused himself.

"I have homework," he declared. He went back into the house!

Tamika shook her head. She wrinkled her brow and shrugged. "Alex confuses me sometimes. It's like he's a puzzle I can't get."

Nonnie asked, "Tamika, are you keeping something about Alex from me"?

Nonnie waited. It was true. Tamika had a secret.

The problem was, she promised Alex she would not share.

Alex was sad at times. It started during the quarantine*, when he couldn't spend time with his friends and the people he loved.

Since his stepmom is a nurse in an emergency department, she was working in the hospital during the lockdown*. At times, she took care of very sick patients. To keep Alex and his sister Alisha safe, she moved in with her sister.

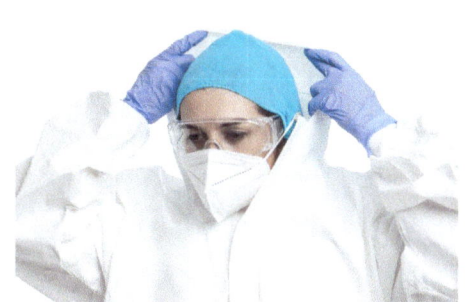

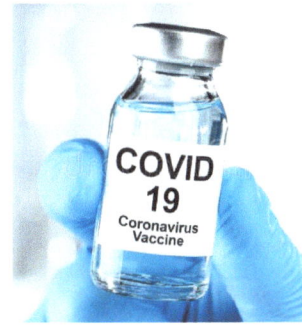

Until she received the vaccine*, Alex only saw her virtually*. This was difficult for everyone, but especially for Alex's little sister Alisha. He spent all his spare time playing with her to distract her from feeling badly about missing her mom.

Although both Alex and Tamika earn great grades, Alex really did not like learning online. He learns best in person.

Plus, Alex couldn't see Tamika and Nonnie except online!

It helped to spend time online with his friends from the Teen Center and Nonnie.

It was good to connect, but he was still sad.

*See *Nonnie Talks about Quarantine* for more.

Things were better now, but Alex developed a new feeling during the pandemic*— anxiety*. He felt nervous*. Sometimes he felt afraid.

Alex's anxiety made him worry*.

He told Tamika how he felt, because she is his best friend, but he made her promise to tell no one….not even Nonnie!

Especially Nonnie. He didn't want to disappoint her.

Alex tried to be pretend everything was okay. It was like he wore a happy mask to cover his anxiety and sorrow. He thought he needed to be strong.

He heard some adults say people need to 'shake off' feelings of depression. He even overheard some adults saying people who saw a counselor were weak*.

Alex did NOT want to be weak!

He wanted to be strong and powerful!

Tamika thought about her secret when Alex left.

Nonnie hoped Alex would return. He never cared about homework this much!

Nonnie asked, "Tamika, are you keeping something from me"?

Tamika looked miserable. She just nodded.

Nonnie said, "Did Alex ask you not to tell me?"

Tamika looked even more miserable, "Yea," she said.

Nonnie understood. Alex was getting older. It would be common for him to want to take care of himself. She said softly, "I won't ask you to break a promise unless someone is in danger."

Tamika thought a minute. She knew Nonnie remembered how much Alex hated the lockdown, but it was over. Tamika thought *Alex is acting weird, but he's okay, right?* "Thanks, Nonnie," she said. "I'm sure Alex is not in danger." She thought, *I'm gonna tell Alex I'm telling Nonnie. It's the right thing to do.*

Nonnie looked into Tamika's eyes and said, "If Alex is in danger, promise me you'll tell me."
Tamika promised.
Nonnie said, "I trust you. Now, let's answer your questions about Josh and LeBron."

Nonnie was thinking.
She remembered when both Alex and Tamika were sad in the past.
They always talked with her.
She imagined them sharing with her now. Nonnie was a good listener.

Nonnie knew these young people well. She sensed something was off with Alex.

She decided to spend time with Alex alone.

For now, Nonnie focused on Tamika's unanswered questions. "Tamika," she said, "You wanted to know why Josh wouldn't go to counseling."

Tamika remembered. She thought about the way Alex hid his feelings during the lockdown, like he wore a mask.

"I think I know," Tamika said. "I think people may be afraid to admit they need help."

"Very wise, Tamika," Nonnie said. "Few people hesitate to get help for a physical problem*, but many people are afraid to get help for a mental health problem*."

Tamika was puzzled. She wasn't sure what Nonnie meant, so she said. "Give me an example, Nonnie."

Nonnie said, "If a person breaks a leg, they go to a doctor to get it fixed. No one expects anyone to limp around on a broken leg. No one says "get better on your own" or "shake it off" for a broken leg. Physical problems are respected."

Tamika understood. "But mental problems can't be seen. They are invisible*."

"Exactly," said Nonnie. "Stigma* around mental health can keep people from seeking help." Nonnie thought a moment. "Treatment for mental illness* isn't the same as a cast or splint on a broken leg, either. It's not as visible*. And, some people think counseling doesn't help."

"What do counselors do, Nonnie?" Tamika was curious, as always.

"Counselors help people sort things out." Nonnie said, "I've always thought of a counselor as a feelings doctor."

"Do counselors listen like you do, Nonnie?" Tamika asked.

"Always," Nonnie smiled. "Listening is first."

Tamika thought for a long time.

Nonnie waited.

Finally, she said, "Something about Josh's roommate upset Alex."

Nonnie agreed. "We need to help him share," she said.

Tamika said, "I think I know why Josh took the pills. He forgot he was worthy."

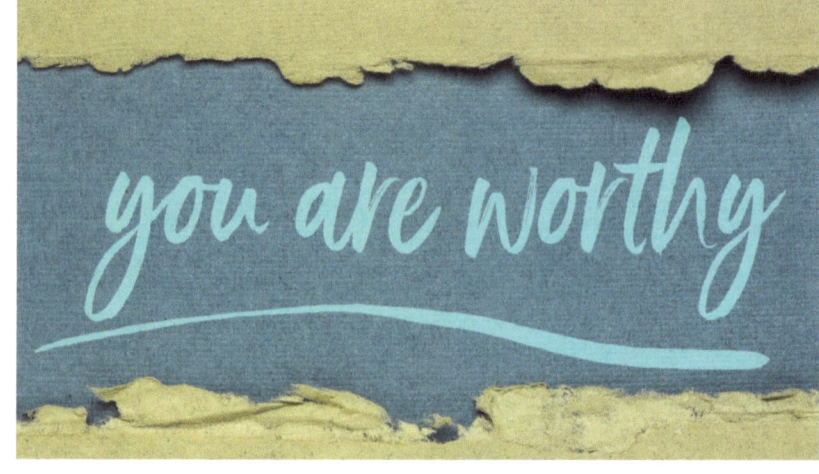

Nonnie was speechless. Before she could respond, Tamika added, "Not forgot exactly. Maybe he couldn't find his way back from his depression."

Nonnie hugged Tamika again, then said, "I love the way you think, honey."

Tamika beamed. "Why is my brother sad."

Nonnie said, "LeBron may feel like many people feel when someone they care about is very depressed. He is working through his feelings about finding Josh."

"He did the right thing," Tamika said. "He was a good friend."

"He did," Nonnie agreed, "but LeBron is probably wondering what he could have done to help Josh."

"It wasn't LeBron's fault, Nonnie," she said, suddenly thinking of Alex. "Let's talk about how we can know when our friends are depressed. I want Alex to be here when you talk about it with us, though."

Just then, Tamika's mom called to pick her up. Tamika's parents wanted to talk with her. When Tamika left, Nonnie called Alex to the porch to sit with her.

Alex's body language helped Nonnie know he wasn't himself.

His shoulders were slumped. He didn't look at her. He held his face in his hands.

Nonnie waited, sitting beside him.

Finally, Alex sighed. "I didn't want to talk with Tamika here," he said. "I made her promise."

Nonnie didn't ask about the promise. She nodded and waited. Alex said, "I don't know how to start, Nonnie."

Nonnie said gently, "You can say anything to me, Alex. Anything at all. Start where ever you wish. You can't disappoint me."

Alex nodded, still looking down. He whispered, "I was afraid I might. Disappoint you."

Nonnie shook her head. "Never," she said. "My love for you means I will offer you acceptance* all of your life!"

Nonnie waited until Alex said, "I told you how sad and lonely I was during the lockdown."

Nonnie said, "I remember. Are you feeling differently now?"

Alex was silent. Then he walked to Nonnie's chalkboard and drew this picture.

Nonnie smiled. "This is how you feel about last year," she said.

Alex sighed and said, "It *was* how I felt. It helped when I talked with you and my mom and dad. It's just….I don't want to…." he paused, looking at Nonnie. His eyes were very sad.

Nonnie understood. She said, "There's nothing you could ever do to take away my love for you, Alex. Nothing. I'm your Nonnie."

Alex buried his head in Nonnies' chest and started to cry. When he was calmer, he said, "What Josh did scared me. What if…"

Nonnie waited so long she wondered how much time had past.

Finally, Alex said, "I got scared because I wonder…if I get ever feel depressed again…would I try to take my own life like Josh?"

Alex's voice became a soft breath. "Suicide*," he said. "So scary."

Nonnie continued holding him. After some time passed, she asked gently, "Do you know why I told you I accepted you, Alex?"

Alex shook his head.

"Do you remember last year when you planted tomato plants for my garden?"

Alex remembered, but had no idea how tomato plants connected to acceptance.

Nonnie smiled. "You started with a tiny seed."
Alex nodded.

"What did you use to nurture the tiny seed?" Nonnie asked.

"Good dirt," Alex said. "You called it soil*. It wasn't just dirt. We put nutrients* in the soil so the seed could grow."

Nonnie smiled. "The seed knew how to grow into the tomato plant. It needed the soil to release its growth."

Chapter Four: Trusted Adults

"We grew big tomatoes," Alex said, smiling.

"We did," said Nonnie. "See, Alex, when an adult accepts a young person, they are like the soil. The young person knows how to grow, just as the seed does. Like the soil enables* the seed's growth, an adult's acceptance releases a young person's growth."

Alex murmured, "What if a young person doesn't have an adult who cares?"

"A great question, Alex," Nonnie agreed. "How can a young person find a trusted adult."

Alex smiled. "I know. Tamika and I did a project for social studies. We listed all the adults who support people our age. Hilary drew pictures of the adults."

Alex pulled up their PowerPoint on his tablet and showed her a picture. "Hilary drew this" he said."

Nonnie said, "Wow, she really is talented!"

Alex downloaded another illustration from their project. "Hilary didn't draw Tamika or me. She just drew some people she created."

Nonnie said, "I'm impressed. There are many kinds of trusted adults in those pictures."
She sighed. "If I ran the universe," she said, "every young person would be able to connect with a trusted adult."

Are there trusted adults in your lives? Maybe the adult who is reading this book with you is one?

Can you name at least two types of trusted adults from the pictures on pages 26 and 27? Write them here:

Trusted adults on page 26
1.
2.

Trusted adults on page 27
1.
2.

Who are your trusted adults?

Alex murmured, "You've always been a trusted adult who loves me, Nonnie. I don't know why I didn't share my feelings with you right away." Nonnie gently said, "Because you're human. None of us is perfect. Neither am I."

Then she asked Alex if he thought about ending his life now and he said, "NO!" firmly.

Nonnie asked if he felt suicidal* during the lockdown, and he was quiet a moment, then said softly, "No, because I knew people loved me. Tamika always made me laugh!"

Nonnie said, "Think of this, Alex. Suicide is a permanent solution to a temporary problem*. Your problems during lockdown got better, right?" Alex's eyes opened wide. "I get it, Nonnie," he said.

The more they talked, the more Alex's fear about Josh made sense to Nonnie. He knew what depression felt like, even though he didn't think about ending his life. The idea of being out of control was frightening to him.

Nonnie explained a lot of young people felt sad and lonely during the lockdown.

"Not just me?" Alex asked.
"Not at all," Nonnie said. "Why do you think they felt sad?"

Alex knew the answer. "Everything changed quickly. Sports stopped. School stopped. I couldn't see you or Tamika in person. It was easy to feel isolated*."

Nonnie agreed. "Adults were worried, too. No one knew what would happen next."

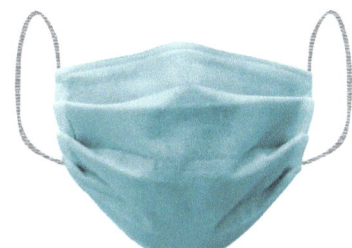

Alex said, "For me, it got better when we could return to school. I could see Tamika and you, Nonnie. I didn't even mind wearing a mask, as long as I could leave the house!"

Nonnie agreed. "I spoke with your stepmom. She said she and her co-workers felt alone, just like many young people."

Nonnie got permission to share Alex's fears with his dad. The three of them talked until past Alex's bedtime. It seemed Alex felt better, but they all agreed to check in often. Alex promised to share if he felt sad again.

The next day, Nonnie picked up Alex and Tamika and took them to the beach. It was a beautiful Saturday. Nonnie knew they would love walking beside the ocean.

Tamika said, "There's something about being at the ocean. It's easy to relax." Alex and she exchanged looks.

Alex said, "Nonnie, I talked with mom and dad last night. I talked with LeBron. I talked with Tamika. I feel a lot better!"

Nonnie was thrilled!

"Talking with trusted adults is the right thing to do," Nonnie smiled. "I spoke with your parents and LeBron last night, Tamika. LeBron agreed to see a counselor at school to sort out his feelings. Josh will be seeing a counselor when he is released from the hospital."

Alex took a big breath and let it out. "I don't understand why I got so afraid."

Tamika poked at his upper arm. "Because you're human, duh?" She grinned. "We have an idea, Nonnie. You were going to tell us the signs of serious depression. What did you call it?"

"Clinical depression," Nonnie said. "I'd love to hear your idea."

Alex smiled, "We talked about this last night. We have a few friends who experienced depression, anxiety or another mental challenge*. Do you think they would be willing to talk with us?"

"A perfect idea, as long as we protect their feelings and privacy!" Nonnie said. "I'm so very proud of you."

Alex dug his toes into the sand and his smile reached his eyes. Tamika thought he looked adorable. He said, "I know one sign. LeBron said Josh slept an awful lot."

Nonnie said, "Yes. Sleep changes can be red flags*."

Chapter Five: Teens Helping Teens

"What's a red flag," Alex asked."

Nonnie smiled. "Red flags warn of danger. At the ocean, a red flag may signify dangerous waves. In mental health, red flags are things caring people should look for when someone seems depressed. Some people are like Josh and they can't seem to get out of bed, while others are awake all night."

"What are other signs, Nonnie?" Tamika asked. "My mom and dad said it's good if friends support each other."

Nonnie said, "Your parents are correct. Did you know they helped me with the Yellow Ribbon Program* to teach teens how to support other teens and get help for them? Before you two were born!" Both Alex and Tamika were surprised. "Tell us," Alex said.

"The project uses yellow ribbons as symbols to encourage connection. We talked about asking for help. We gave out cards and taught teens how to get help for others."

Tamika said, "Like Peer Education!"
"In some ways," Nonnie said. "Another red flag may be pulling away from others*. People may fail to take care of themselves physically or neglect* their responsibilities*."

See Appendix on page 80

Tamika and Alex were quiet. They were thinking.

Alex said, "One of my problems was the way I thought during the lockdown. I kept thinking, over and over—*when will this end?*"

Tamika said, "I thought the same thing!"

Alex nodded. "I guess most people did. I was obsessed* with it, though. It became hard to make a decision."

Tamika gasped. "I remember! You could not decide what you wanted to do when we were virtual. I'd suggest we stream a movie and you'd just shrug."

Alex mumbled, "I just felt tired. And moody*."

Nonnie walked them to a restaurant along the shore and ordered them whatever they wanted. They talked as they ate.
Alex was hungry! So was Tamika! Nonnie knew it was easier to talk when young people feel safe and aren't hungry! She said, "Please remember each person is different. People may be moody or show other signs without being depressed.

Nonnie asked Alex, "What made you feel better?"
He answered, "The lockdown ended!"

Nonnie smiled, "If you ever feel those things again…"
Alex interrupted with a big grin, "I'll tell you both," he said

What do YOU Think?

Nonnie taught Tamika and Alex some signs of depression. There are other signs. *

Talk with a trusted adult. How does talking about depression make you feel? Do you know a friend who felt depressed? What did you do?

Please draw or write your thoughts here:

See Appendix on page 72

Chapter Six: An Unexpected Surprise

The day at the beach was a good day for Alex and Tamika and each day was better.

Nonnie was teaching and writing a textbook. She saw them a lot.
School and activities were happening again.
LeBron finished his internship and was planning his wedding!
He was accepted to law school! Josh was feeling better.

Then...did you ever notice how life can change quickly?

Nonnie was diagnosed* with breast cancer*. One minute she seemed fine, and the next she was in the hospital. She had surgery right away. Alex called Tamika and they went to the hospital when Nonnie was able to go home.

The first thing Nonnie did was reassure* Tamika and Alex.

She told them she was okay. She explained it is important to get testing to find out if a person has cancer. She said the word cancer didn't scare her. She said the cancer was small and it was found early. She would be fine.

Alex said, "I want you to be okay forever, Nonnie." Tamika agreed.

Nonnie hugged them both. "Forever is a long time, loves, but I am happy to be with you now. I trust my doctors and I'm ready to do whatever treatment I need." She paused, thinking about how sensitive these two fine young people were. "One of the treatments I will need is called chemotherapy*. I will be given drugs to help my body fight the cancer."

Tamika frowned. "I don't like the sound of drugs. Will they make you sick?"

Alex was quiet. Nonnie smiled at him, then said, "Well, a side effect* of the chemo* is I will lose my hair." Alex looked angry. Tamika looked upset. Nonnie knew just what to do. She invited Tamika, Alex and Alisha to her house. They tried on her wigs* and chemo caps*. They ate pizza. They talked about their fears. They finally laughed!

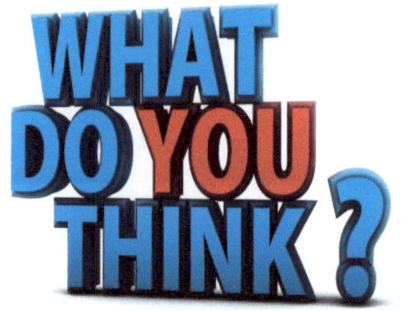

What do YOU Think?

Alex and his sister Alisha wish Nonnie did not need treatment for cancer. Tamika feels the same way.

Do you know anyone in your life who needs to deal with cancer? Is the word cancer a scary word for you? Share your feelings about cancer with a trusted adult.

Please draw or write your thoughts here:

Nonnie watched Alex. She was concerned about his mental health. Would he become depressed again?

Nonnie is lucky.

She has a wonderful friend who is a psychologist*.
His name is Dr. Bob.

Nonnie knew how tough it is to take care of a mental health challenge with someone you love very much. She wanted Dr. Bob's perspective*. She knew she should not be Alex's counselor. They are too close to one another.

Dr. Bob lives far away, so they had a virtual meeting together.

Dr. Bob was very helpful. He is a kind, caring counselor.
He agreed with Nonnie. If Alex became depressed, Nonnie should not be his counselor.

Before she started her treatments, Nonnie invited Tamika and Alex to spend time with her. Dr. Bob suggested she might be able to figure out how they were handling her diagnosis.

Nonnie once imagined comforting Tamika and Alex. Now, it was true. Both Alex and Tamika seemed sad.

Nonnie knew sad was okay. They didn't want her to be sick. Were they more than just sad, though?

Dr. Bob said Nonnie should continue watching for the red flags she knew from the DSM (Diagnostic and Statistical Manual of Mental Disorders)** and remember the keys to any behavior* were two things:

1. Did the feeling or behavior happen again and again? Another way to say it would be persistent* (happening nearly every day)?
2. Was the feeling or behavior consistent*? Did it remain the same over time?

See Appendix on page 72

Dr. Bob encouraged* Nonnie to help Alex seek counseling.
He said, "The central part of the word encouragement is courage*. It takes courage to support young people and it takes courage to seek help as a young person."

Nonnie agreed. "It feels like Alex is caught up in fear. He worries he will be seen as weak if he talks to a counselor."

Dr. Bob's warmth oozed through the zoom. He smiled and said, "When people want to avoid counseling and say to me, "Why can't I just talk to myself, why do I need to talk to someone else"? I say that's a pretty universal thought, but, much like starting a jigsaw puzzle, the first step to mental health is to lay all the pieces out on the table and turn them face-side-up. A counselor has experience helping others put together puzzles before and can help in the process."

"A great way to look at counseling!" Nonnie loved the idea of a puzzle.

Dr. Bob smiled, "Yes. And four hands are better than two."
He reminded Nonnie the words psychotherapy*, therapy* and counseling all mean the same thing, and counseling is the least scary word.

Nonnie said, "Thank you for your wisdom, my friend. Do you have any other analogies* I can use to encourage Alex?"

Dr. Bob said, "Sometimes I use the analogy of going to the barber or hairdresser. We cannot see the back of our own head. A second mirror will be held behind us so we can see our head from a different perspective. What I hope happens in counseling is someone saying, "Aha, now I see it!"

Nonnie smiled. "Thank you, Bob. I will stay in touch."

Nonnie made sure Alex's parents—his mom, his dad, and his step-mom—were careful to watch his behavior and listen to him.

Her best ally was Tamika.

Tamika and Alex spent time together since they were toddlers. They had helped each other through many challenges.

They were outstanding friends.
Nonnie thought about the Yellow Ribbon Program she taught. Young people often show their true feelings to their peers.
Yes, Tamika would be a great help.

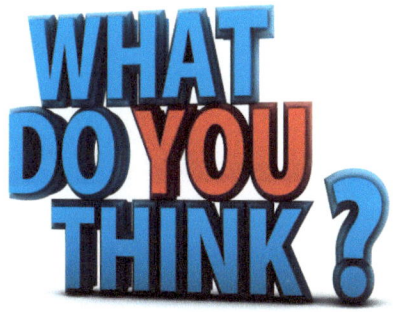

What do YOU Think?

Dr. Bob's wisdom helped Nonnie.

What did you think of his analogy about the jigsaw puzzle?

Did you think the barber and hairdresser analogy for counseling makes sense? Why or why not?

Please draw or write your thoughts here:

Chapter Seven: Is Alex Sad?

Nonnie thanked Dr. Bob and promised to keep in touch. She made sure Alex's parents—his mom, his dad, and his stepmom—were careful to watch his behavior and listen to him.

All the adults knew Alex and Tamika were in the middle of puberty**, so mood swings were likely.

They watched for other signs, listening to Dr. Bob's wisdom. After a few months of chemo, Nonnie's blood counts* changed. She needed to be protected from infection*. It was a little like the quarantine*. She needed to stay isolated until her blood work was better and she was less likely to get sick.

Alex did NOT like only visiting with her virtually again!

Even his sister Alisha noticed he seemed unhappy.

*See *Nonnie Talks about Puberty* for more information.

She said to her dad and mom, "Something's wrong with my Alex!"

Alisha loves her big brother a lot.

Nonnie spoke with Alex's mom, stepmom, and dad.
She talked with Tamika's mom and dad. The adults made a plan!

Then, in a few weeks, Nonnie received good news. Her blood counts improved! She could meet with people face to face! Nonnie invited Tamika and Alex to her house for lunch.
She wore a chemo cap.

Nonnie laughed and told the children she likes caps better than wigs. When she wears wigs they always seem to shift on her head and she can't see! Tamika and Nonnie laughed. Alex just smiled. While they were having tea, Nonnie said, "Alex, you don't seem happy."

A minute ago, Alex was calm. When Nonnie asked him if he was happy, he jumped up, went into the living room, and looked very angry!

Tamika followed him and sat down without talking. She was holding space with him.

Nonnie followed.
She sat down beside Tamika.

She was also holding space. She didn't talk or ask Alex why he was angry. She didn't give him advice. Nonnie and Tamika simply stayed with him.

After a few minutes, Alex sighed. He took several deep breaths and said, "Why do I always need to be happy?"

Nonnie smiled. "You don't always need to be happy, Alex. No one is happy all the time. You seem sadder than usual, though."

Alex blurted out. "I hate cancer!" Tamika said, "Me too!"

Nonnie waited, then finally Alex said, "I think I'm feeling depressed again, Nonnie."

Nonnie said softly, "I am so proud of you. Acknowledging your feelings takes a lot of courage." She smiled. "I have two wonderful friends and colleagues who are psychologists*."

Chapter Eight: Counseling

Nonnie continued, "My friend Dr. Bob lives far away, but the other has an office near us, Alex. I think you'll like him. May I call him and bring you to his office? He can decide if counseling would help you feel better."

"Right now?!" Alex sputtered.
Before Nonnie could speak, Tamika said, "Not right now, silly. It's a Sunday!" They all laughed, even Alex.

Nonnie asked Alex how he felt, and he shared his sadness was not as big as during the lockdown. Nonnie nodded, "You're not in crisis*." she said. "I'll call Dr. Rueben and set up an appointment after I talk with your parents. Is this OK with you?"

Alex muttered, "Yeah," and Tamika said, "I'm glad. I'll go with you." Alex smiled. He always felt better when Tamika was with him

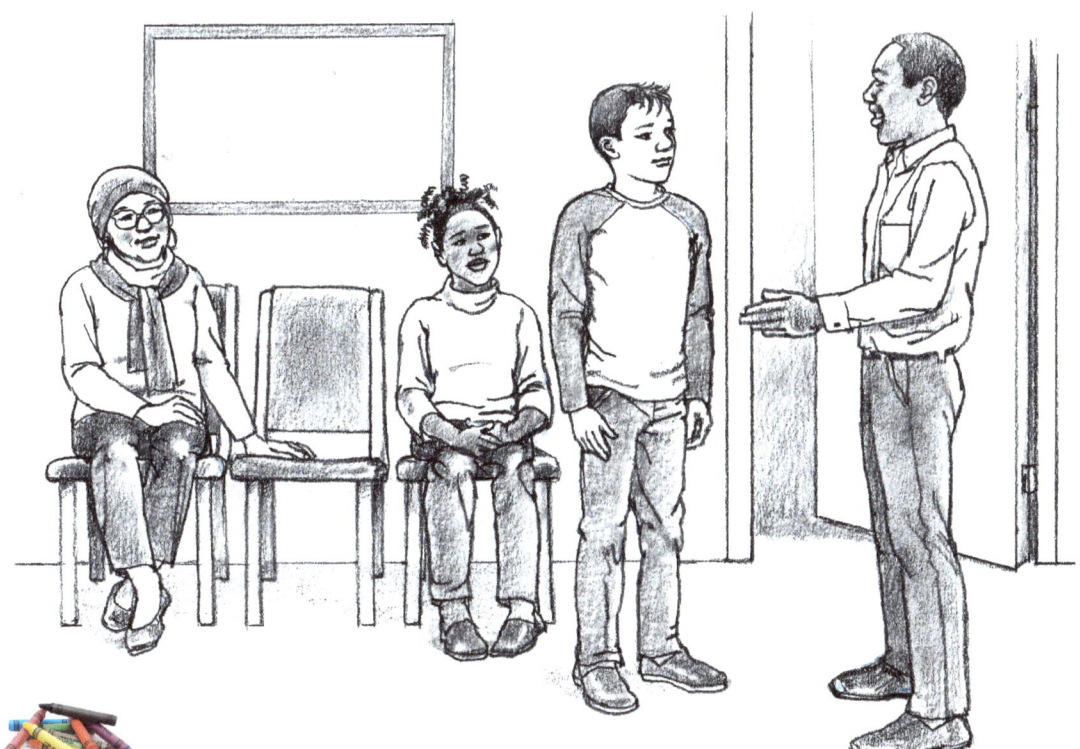

Next week, they went to Dr. Rueben's office.

Alex did like him right away.

Nonnie and Tamika waited while they spoke.

Dr. Rueben's office was warm and inviting. He settled into a soft chair and invited Alex to join him on a sofa. They would be close enough to talk easily, but not too close to make Alex uncomfortable.

Alex looked around the room. It didn't look like his idea of a psychologist's office. There was no couch like in the movies. This room wasn't much different from his living room at home.

Alex perched on the very end of the sofa and held onto the sofa's arm with one hand. His other hand was rolled into a fist.
Dr. Rueben could tell Alex was apprehensive* about seeing him for counseling.

Dr. Rueben was warm, caring, and gentle. He didn't ask Alex why he came to see him. In fact, to Alex's surprise, he didn't ask about depression or feeling sad.
Dr. Rueben didn't ask about his feelings at all!

Instead, Dr. Rueben said, "Alex, I'd like to get to know you. Tell me about you."

Dr. Rueben sensed Alex was hesitant. He could tell Alex was not into seeing him, as if it were someone else's idea.

Alex looked confused. He was prepared for personal questions. He expected Dr. Rueben to make him explain how he felt.

After a while, Alex said, "I play Minecraft."

Dr. Rueben smiled. "I rocked at Pac-Man!"

Alex fought a smile, holding it back hard. "Tamika and me play Mario Odyssey. At the Center, we sometimes play Among Us."

Dr. Rueben's smile was welcoming. He looked at ease, and leaned a tiny bit towards Alex. He didn't make eye contact constantly. Alex had been afraid he might. He laughed. "I'm getting older! I know about Mario but not the other two games."

Alex shrugged. "We have a vintage video game console at the Teen Center. I like Pac-Man."

Dr. Rueben nodded and said, "I'm into music. Are you?"

Alex released his tightly clenched fingers from the sofa's arm. "I really love music," he said.

Dr. Rueben said, "I like jazz, but I enjoy all music."

Alex almost forgot why he was there. "Right now I'm into Drake. And The Weekend. Lil Baby and Gym Class Heroes are cool."

Dr. Rueben grinned. "Now I really feel old."

"You're not old," Alex said. "Nonnie is a whole lot older."

Alex felt less worried as he talked with Dr. Rueben. He didn't even notice when he relaxed his fist. He started leaning towards Dr. Rueben—just a little bit.

Finally, Alex said, "I don't think I need counseling."

Dr. Rueben nodded. "Counseling isn't what people think it is. I am a trusted adult who can help you sort through your feelings"

Alex said, "I know about trusted adults. My Nonnie taught me. I have a great family. And Tamika." Then, he thought about the times when they all got together, when his sister was a baby, before the lockdown and when his parents were less busy.

Alex missed those days.

Dr. Rueben agreed. "You do have a great family. Sometimes young people come to me when they need more than family."

Then, Dr. Rueben asked, "What would it feel like if you felt better, Alex? Can you imagine it?"

Alex thought about Nonnie's cancer, then said, "Like taking a heavy backpack off my shoulders."

Dr. Rueben's smile was comforting. He said, "What if I tell you we can get you there?"

The session with Dr. Rueben was over! The time went fast. Alex thought about how much he didn't want to burden Nonnie. Maybe talking with Dr. Rueben could help….

Dr. Rueben and Alex joined Nonnie and Tamika in another office. He said, "I enjoyed meeting Alex."
Alex added softly. "I'd like to see Dr. Rueben again."

Both Nonnie and Tamika were happy. Nonnie had changed into a wig at Tamika's urging. She told Nonnie she looked beautiful!

Dr. Rueben continued, "I'd like Alex and I to continue talking. I can be an outlet where Alex can sort out feelings." Dr. Rueben spoke directly to Alex. "Remember, it's not a failure if people go to a counselor."

Everyone thanked Dr. Rueben. Tamika said, "Let's go to my house so I can beat you at Mario." Alex grinned. "Wanna bet?"

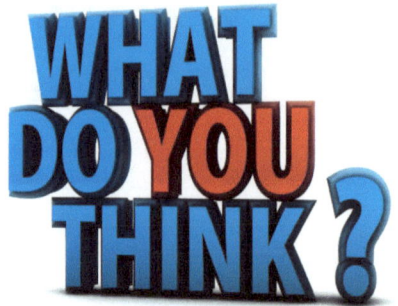

What do YOU Think?

Counseling is one way to help someone with mental illness feel better and be mentally healthy.

Do you know anyone who saw a counselor?
Have you? What do you know about counseling?
If a counselor was like Dr. Rueben, would you feel safe?
Why or why not? What is your best idea of a counselor?

Please draw or write your thoughts here:

Chapter Eight: Learning from Others

While listening to Dr. Rueben, Nonnie realized something she needed to call out* with Alex and Tamika. She needed to discuss the elephant in the room* - the thing no one was talking about but was important! She needed to talk about death*.

Nonnie told Tamika and Alex a story about her early years as a nurse. She worked in pediatric oncology* and cared for many children dealing with cancer. She learned a lot about life and death while taking care of them.

"I was 23," Nonnie said. "The experience changed me. I realized everyone dies. I began to see each day as a gift. I started choosing to do things I loved and found people I loved to share my days."

Tamika said, "You sure do love teaching, Nonnie."
Alex added, "You love us." He hugged Nonnie really hard.
"How did working with sick and dying children change you?"

Nonnie smiled. "I realized I needed to live my life one day at a time*. If I'm anxious about something that might happen in the future, I lose the joy of today."

Alex looked at Tamika shyly, then said, "I like spending my days with you." Tamika grinned. "Of course. Me too. Alex, you're so weird."

*See *Nonnie Talks about Death* for more.

Nonnie thought about Tamika and Alex's idea when they first spoke about LeBron's sadness. She knew Peer Educators who could help them learn about mental health and mental illness. She spoke with a few teens who were very helpful. The first person Nonnie called was a friend of Tamika's named Hilary.

Hilary shared how alone she felt when she was hiding the unwanted touch** she experienced when she was younger. She shared how she felt as if a huge weight was lifted when she disclosed*. She talked about how her counselor helped her realize what happened was not her fault.

Hilary said, "I see my counselor every month now and can connect with her in between sessions if I want. She tells me I may feel strong memories when I have a partner* or even when I have a baby some day. I trust her. Seeing her saved my life."

Alex asked only one question. "Hilary," he said, "thank you for helping me. Do you think it's OK to talk with someone about your mental health?"

Hilary said, "So much." Tamika hugged them both.

*See *Nonnie Talks about Consent* for more.

Then, they spoke with Kendle*. Kendle was Alex's crush but, after they went to a dance and time passed, they grew apart. Now they were good friends. Kendle had a new crush.

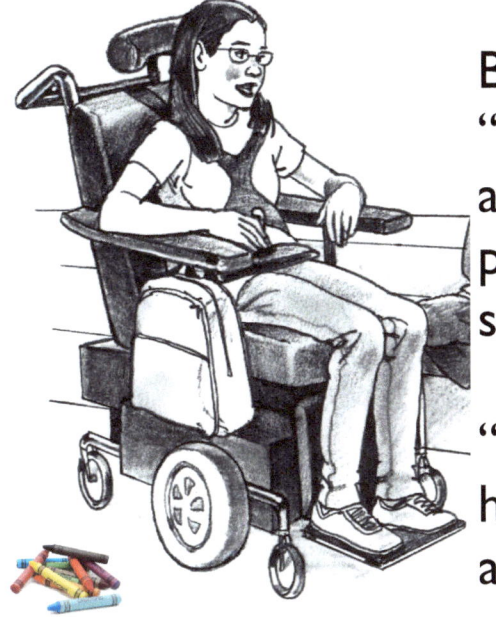

Before Kendle started talking, Alex said, "Kendle, I'm sorry. My emotions* have been all over the place. I'm afraid I wasn't a good partner." Alex looked miserable and Kendle spoke up quickly.

"Alex," she said, giving him a big smile." We had fun. "We're young. My mom says, at our age, we need to figure out ourselves and who we like. I was just as distracted as you, but with different things." Alex knew Kendle was working on a big project for school. He smiled, relieved.

Nonnie said, "We're talking about mental health. How do you stay mentally healthy, Kendle?"

Kendle smiled. "I keep busy with things I enjoy. I spend time every day doing breathing and relaxation. I make sure I surround myself with people who get me and I love." She shrugged. "I'm not happy all the time, but I mostly am."

Tamika glanced at Alex. He gave her an encouraging nod. She said, "When Nonnie got sick, Alex was worried she would die."

Alex's smile was huge and was just for Tamika.

*For more of Kendle's story, see *Nonnie Talks about Disability*.

Kendle was very supportive. "I've had a lot of physical health issues since I was born, Alex," she said gently. "My family has always been alert to my mental health. They help me take one day at a time."

Tamika said, "Nonnie, you tell us you take one day at a time!"

Nonnie smiled and nodded.

Tamika and Alex were talking together while they walked to Nonnie's car. They thought of something.

Alex said, "Do you remember when you brought us to one of the classes you teach at the college?"
Nonnie remembered.

Tamika said, "You were teaching about healthy relationships and one of your students talked about his childhood."

"I remember," Nonnie said. "He shared about his life in foster care* until he was adopted*."

"He said his birth parents were addicted* to heroin* and he was removed from them as a baby." Tamika said.

Alex said, "I thought he was very brave. He talked about learning about the disease* of addiction*. He said his adopted parents were his real parents who raised him."

Tamika added, "He shared he'd been to counseling when he was first adopted. He said he still saw his counselor when he felt stressed."

"All of this is true," Nonnie said. "He's finishing medical school!"

Tamika said, "Seems there are many reasons to see a counselor!"

Alex wanted to talk with another person. When they were younger, a friend named Annie got in trouble because she sent a graphic* pic on her phone. Tamika and he got in trouble too.*

Nonnie called Annie and they talked.

Annie told them how seeing a counselor helped her understand the "why"* of her behavior.

Nonnie was pleased. "It's very important to help young people figure out why they do things that get them into trouble," she said. "Behavior doesn't just happen."

*For more of Annie's story, see Nonnie Talks about Sex.

Annie said, "I realized giving in to peer pressure* doesn't buy love or friends." She laughed. "You two are better friends to me now than any people I thought were my friends when I sent the pic. Counseling helped me."

Alex hesitated, then asked a question as respectfully as he could. "Did you want to go to counseling, Annie?"

Annie shook her head. "School made me go, but I'm so glad I did."

Later, they spoke with another friend. Their friend Darius lost his father in a car accident when he was only eight years old. His mom married his step-dad when he was ten.

Alex said, "I have a stepmom. My parents got divorced. I didn't like her at first, but I love her now."

Darius was kind. He said, "I don't know what it's like to live through a divorce. I do remember losing my dad. My mom took me to counseling right away."
"Did it help?" asked Tamika.

"So much," Darius said. "My mom was sad enough. It helped to talk with someone else. When she remarried, we went to family counseling together."

"Thank you, Darius," Nonnie said. "Grief* is hard. I'm glad you're doing well."

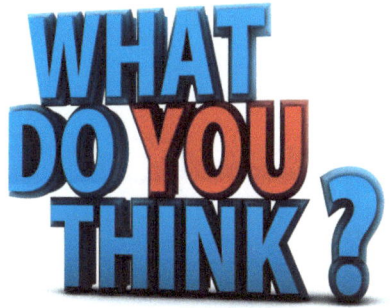

What do YOU Think?

Tamika and Alex's friends were open and honest. They wanted to help.

In the next chapter, Alex and Tamika will learn more about trauma. Before you read this chapter, let's talk about triggering. A past trauma or even something seen or read can cause emotional distress. How do you feel about reading about trauma? Talk with a trusted adult.

Please draw or write your thoughts here:

Chapter Nine: Trauma

Alex was quiet after they spoke with their friends.

Tamika studied him for a while. Finally, she said, "Alex, what's bubbling in that grade A brain of yours? Spill!"

Alex smiled. Nonnie noticed how Tamika could usually make Alex happy.

Alex said, "Dr. Rueben said trauma* can cause mental health problems long after it happens. I wonder if I ever figured out my feelings after my mom and dad got divorced."

Nonnie agreed. "It might help to talk about it with Dr. Rueben."

Alex said, "I will!"

Tamika said, "I know! After your session, you can come to my place and we can play video games again." Alex looked happy.

*See Nonnie Talks about Trauma for more.

Then, Tamika looked troubled, and Alex noticed right away. "What's up, Tamika?" He asked, reading her body language.

"I spoke with my Great Uncle Isaac last night. He told me he was in Vietnam with my Abuelito*. He was in the Air Force and my grandpa was a Marine, but they were in-laws, so they connected."

"Are you missing your Abuelito, Tamika?" Alex remembered helping Tamika through her grief.

"Not so much right now. But, my Great Uncle Isaac told me something I didn't know. He said, right after they both returned from the war, my Abuelito wasn't OK mentally. That's all he said." She turned to Nonnie. "I'd like to know more. How do I find out?"

Alex spoke before Nonnie could, "You could ask your grandma. You see her every week or so. I'm sure she will talk with you."

Tamika nodded, "Will you go with me?"
Of course, Alex said he would.

Tamika's grandma told her about PTSD (post traumatic stress disorder)*.

She shared how Tamika's grandpa needed counseling after the war because of the trauma he experienced and saw. Tamika's grandma said, "Counseling helped your Abuelito a lot."

Later, Tamika and Alex researched PTSD and depression*. They often did research projects together for their own knowledge and for Peer Education.

They learned PTSD can be part of any trauma survivor*'s life. It can occur in anyone who experiences a traumatic event, like a serious accident, a terrorist attack, a natural disaster, war/combat, or sexual violence.

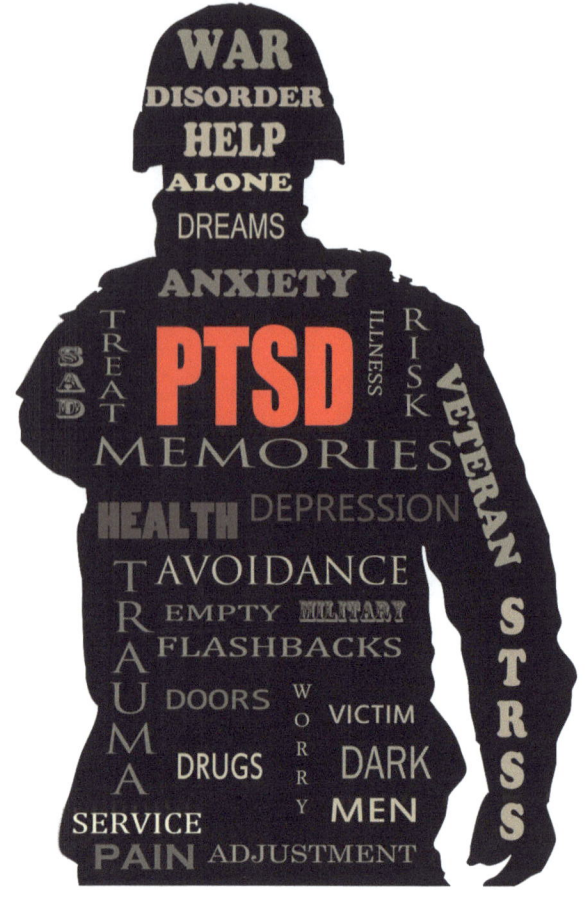

PTSD can cause survivors to relive traumatic events.
They may have nightmares.

Mental health problems can happen right away or even years after the event.

Tamika thought about her Abuelito. He was so gentle with her all her life. He was a musician. He was a great teacher.

He never talked about the war. Her grandma was right. Counseling was good for him.

They were pleased when they discovered many projects created to help prevent veteran suicide.

To read Alex and Tamika's research on depression, see Appendix on page 72

"We can help!" said Tamika. She remembered learning about kinds of trauma, like being bullied or treated badly due to race, gender, sexuality, size, or ability.

Alex agreed. "We learned collective trauma can happen when a group experiences systemic racism** and hate," he said.

Tamika asked. "Remember when we went to Washington DC and saw the African American Museum?"

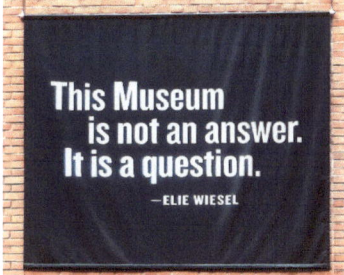

Alex remembered. "We saw the Holocaust Museum, too."

Tamika added, "And the Native American Museum."

"Exposure to violence can cause trauma," added Alex.

"We can have empathy* for others' experiences," said Tamika. "We can educate about trauma and the way it affects people's lives," Alex agreed.

Alex suddenly thought of his cousin. They called Sara and asked her about mental health in the military. Sara told them things were improving, but admitted counseling was frowned upon in the military for many years.

Alex said firmly. "Talking with a counselor doesn't make a person weak!!"

*See *Nonnie Talks about Race* for more information.

Chapter Ten: Learning Together

Tamika and Alex were suddenly very interested in mental health. They asked Nonnie if the Teen Center could host a discussion. The topic* would be mental health challenges.

Nonnie thought it was a great idea. She said, "I will ask Dr. Bob to join us virtually, since he lives in another state, and ask Dr. Rueben to be at the Center."

Alex asked their friends Darius and Annie to attend.

The next Peer Educator meeting, a group of teens gathered to talk.

Tamika and Alex set their typical Peer Educator guidelines of respect*, worthiness*, confidentiality*, and the right to speak or pass*. Nonnie made sure everyone felt safe and honored.

First, Dr. Bob talked with the young people about Goldilocks!

He said, "I'm sure you've heard the fairy tale of Goldilocks.
Think about the message the story gives us about perfection*."

Tamika said, "Perfection? I don't get it."

Dr. Bob laughed, "The porridge is too hot or too cold, the chair is too hard or too soft, the bed is too big or too small.

Goldilocks is searching for something just right—for perfection. In life, there is no such thing as perfection. Whatever we do, we are going to do it a bit too much or not enough. This leads to feelings of inadequacy*." Dr. Bob smiled. "I've heard people say the 'perfect' is the enemy of the 'good'.

Nonnie spoke up, "Yes! When people feel inadequate because they are trying to be perfect, they may doubt themselves." She gave Tamika a big smile. "They may forget their worth."

"I'll give you an example," said Dr. Bob. "A guidance counselor might call a parent to share a young person wrote an essay about suicide. What might a counselor think?'

"I've often wondered what adults at school think!" Tamika said.

Nonnie was surprised when Alex said, "Maybe it's no big deal. It's just an essay and a kid might be curious."

Dr. Bob said, "What other reaction might happen?"

Hilary was brave. She said, "Something like this happened to me. Before I knew it I was in a psychiatric hospital."

Nonnie said, "Sharing took courage, Hilary. We're honored you told us."

Hilary smiled. "Everyone here knew anyway." she looked around at the teens in the Center. "You all were accepting when I returned."

Tamika was curious. "Did they do the right thing, Hilary? If it's not too personal."

Hilary shook her head. "It isn't too personal. Yes, I think they did. I was upset at first. Scared, too. I now know it was the best thing for me. I needed help."

Dr. Bob said, "A great way to return to my Goldilocks story.

None of us are perfect. When a counselor gets a call and assesses* a young person for danger to self, there is no perfect response. I try to make a mistake on the side of safety."

Then, Dr. Bob and Dr. Rueben opened the floor for questions.

Nonnie sat back and listened as Tamika and Alex smoothly took over the roles of facilitators. They'd learned so much together and they were great co-leaders for the group.

Tamika wrote questions on the Teen Center whiteboard.

1. How long does a person need to go to counseling if they're depressed?
2. What is bipolar disorder?
3. What if someone cuts?

Dr. Rueben answered the first question, "Every person is unique*. It depends on the person and what they need."

Alex spoke up. "Seeing a counselor doesn't mean you're weak. It means you are wise enough to get help."

Tamika clapped and Alex looked embarrassed, but then he smiled.

Dr. Bob took the second one. "Bipolar disorder* is a mental health condition affecting how a person feels, thinks and acts. People with bipolar disorder have brains that work differently when they are sick from how they do when they feel well."

A teen named Sam raised a hand. "My dad has bipolar disorder. He takes medicine* now and is better. He used to be depressed sometimes and wildly energetic* other times."

Dr. Rueben said, "I'm glad counseling and medication are helping." He looked at the white board and responded to the third question. "Another way to say cutting* is self-harm*. When people harm themselves, they may be dealing with bad feelings they cannot figure out how to release. My job is to help them find healthier ways to deal with their problems and feelings."

Hilary said, "I met a girl in the hospital who cut herself. She was feeling better when I left. Her mom was upset she was in the hospital. She was afraid someone would judge her parenting."

Dr. Bob said, "The stigma of seeking help for mental illness keeps people from counseling. You are bright young people. Can you think of ways to lower stigma?"

Alex took Tamika's place at the whiteboard. He wrote all the ideas the others called out to him.

1. Educate yourself.
2. Educate others.
3. Raise awareness of the importance of counseling.
4. Encourage equality between mental and physical illnesses.
5. Show kindness and empathy for everyone.
6. Model respect and acceptance.

Dr. Rueben said, "These are wonderful ideas!"

Alex got excited, "Nonnie," he said. "Could we write a Peer Educator lesson on mental health?"

Chapter Eleven: Self-Care for Mental Health

Nonnie said, "Absolutely!"

Sam spoke up, "I have an idea. Some of us are in drama club at school. What if we created a play about raising awareness of the stigma of mental illness?"

Alex added, smiling at Dr. Rueben. "And how counseling is good."

Everyone got excited!

Nonnie said, "I love it! Sam, ask for volunteers from school and the Center. You can write the script and rehearse here. I'll find you audiences!"

Alex said, "Can we talk about how we can help ourselves when we feel sad or anxious?"

Dr. Rueben said, "Meditation is great."

Dr. Bob added, "As is centered breathing and relaxation."

Tamika said, "Nonnie taught us all to relax and center our breathing!"

"Excellent!" Both doctors said at once. Everyone laughed.

Dr. Rueben smiled and said, "Laughter is good, too. We should try not to take ourselves too seriously."

Dr. Bob said, "Eat well. Healthy foods are good fuel."

Dr. Rueben laughed, "So is an occasional pizza!"

Three of the teens cried out together, "Pizza is healthy!"

A senior named Willow said, "Especially with pineapple!"

Everyone else groaned, "Ewwww!"

 Dr. Rueben added, "Exercise helps."

Sam said, "We can do that!"

Dr. Bob said, "Getting a good night's sleep can improve mental health."

 Willow laughed, "We should all sleep like my cat then. She sleeps 24/7."

Nonnie reminded them all, "Supporting each other is a wonderful way to stay connected and not feel alone."

Nonnie said, "I try be aware of my words. I no longer use the word 'crazy'. Instead, I say 'wildly', like "I am wildly busy" when someone asks how many projects I'm working on."

Everyone seemed relaxed and encouraged. Nonnie was glad.

Chapter Twelve: A Healthy Relationship

A few weeks later, Tamika and Alex went to Nonnie's house for a dinner of lasagna and salad. She no longer needed a chemo cap or wig! Her hair was back! It was white. She loved her new color! So did Tamika and Alex.

The original play written by the Teen Center Peer Educators was called *If You Only Knew Me*. They performed it for the end of school assembly and taught about mental health.

Summer was just around the corner.
Tamika and Alex would be very busy. The Teen Center was holding summer camps. They were both facilitators.

Tamika and Alex were happy. Eighth grade would be a good year.

All three of them laughed a lot during the meal.

Tamika and Alex giggled. They stole food from each other's plates and giggled some more.

Both Alex and Tamika were grinning.

Finally, Tamika asked Nonnie, "When you talked about relationships* with us, didn't you tell us it was a good idea to develop a crush on a good friend?"

She winked at Alex, whose face lit up. "We're good friends, Nonnie!" Alex said, beaming. "Don't you think?"

Nonnie wasn't surprised to see them develop from good friends to two young people in a healthy relationship. They were learning about connection. They were honest with each other.

She was really proud of them.
She knew they were great together.

She said, "Today is a good day. The best day ever!"

*See *Nonnie Talks about Relationships* for more.

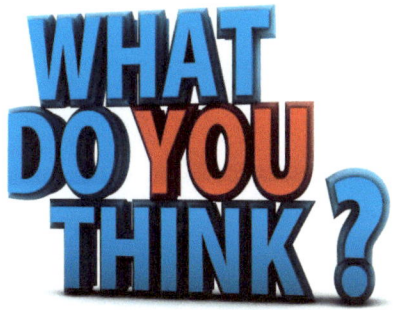

What do YOU Think?

Tamika and Alex learned a lot about mental health.

What was the most important thing you learned about mental health? What is mental health stigma?
Are you surprised Tamika and Alex became a couple? Why or why not?

Please draw or write your thoughts here:

Appendix 1: (Alex and Tamika's Research)

Tamika and Alex wanted to know more about depression. More and more of their friends seem depressed.

They researched Clinical Depression.

Dr. Bob talked about the signs of depression as listed in the DSM (please see the glossary on page 86)

With Nonnie's help, they read the DSM-5 and found that 5 of these 8 symptoms indicate depression:

1. Depressed mood most of the day, nearly every day.
2. Markedly diminished interest or pleasure in all, or almost all, activities most of the day, nearly every day.
3. Significant weight loss when not dieting or weight gain, or decrease or increase in appetite nearly every day.
4. A slowing down of thought and a reduction of physical movement (observable by others, not merely subjective feelings of restlessness or being slowed down).
5. Fatigue or loss of energy nearly every day.
6. Feelings of worthlessness or excessive or inappropriate guilt nearly every day.
7. Diminished ability to think or concentrate, or indecisiveness, nearly every day.
8. Recurrent thoughts of death, the current suicidal ideation without a specific plan, or a suicide attempt or a specific plan for taking one's own life.

Appendix 2: Personal Story from a Young Adult

Max Dolnick, age 23
3/21/21

Back in high school, I had lots of friends, I took honors courses and had (mostly) good grades. I even taught swimming at a summer camp for 4 years. I was able to get into the college of my choice, Towson University. It wasn't easy, I had a lot of challenges and needed help to achieve these successes, but I had a plan and a path.

When I was 19 and a freshman at college, I started to experience a lot of symptoms of anxiety and depression. I was uncomfortable and felt almost painful restlessness and agitation. Like I was pent up. I stopped going to classes. I cut myself off from friends. I even stopped eating. I was having suicidal thoughts. I finally realized I had a problem and that I needed help. I reached out to the counseling center at school and we worked out that I was not able to complete my first semester and I went home to seek further help and began to commit myself to getting better.

My life has taken a different path than what I expected. I try not to worry about making comparisons to other people. You don't have to understand the details of someone's mental illness to connect with it. If someone is in pain – physical or mental pain – everyone experiences these things. Not just people with mental illness.

No matter who you are, you have the ability to take control of your life. Even if you feel powerless. You can make the smallest decisions to make change. Start off small. Today I will take a shower. Today I will whatever, call a friend. And those decision will change your life. Just stay committed to getting better.

Thank you, Max, for your courageous words. You will help other young people. Love, Nonnie

Appendix 3: Artwork from Young People

"Untitled" Jake Comatas, age 19, Pages 74—76

Appendix 3: Artwork from Young People

Appendix 3: Artwork from Young People

Appendix 3: Artwork from Young People

"Perspective" Elle Free, age 18

Appendix 3: Artwork from Young People

"Words Hurt" Willow Maffio, age 17

Appendix 4: Food for Thought

Author's Note:

Writing *Nonnie Talks about Mental Health* was bittersweet.

I didn't plan to write another Nonnie book after my first, but the children I taught and the parents who reached out to me with positive comments inspired me.

Left alone, I doubt I would stop writing these books that are a true labor of love.

My amazing artist, Alice Burroughs, told me she wanted to retire from illustrating Tamika and Alex and Nonnie after my 9th book, and I respected her wishes. Then, the pandemic changed our lives. I responded to the closure of our Common Ground Teen Center on 3/16/2020 by holding twice daily virtual meetings with young people. Those wonderful experiences morphed into ten free virtual summer camps for 12-14 year-olds; I personally logged 1100 Zoom hours in June-July of 2020.

I was concerned for the mental health of the young people I serve from the start. My daily virtual contact with them reinforced their need. I sought out Alice to request illustrations for *Nonnie Talks about Quarantine*, which she graciously donated. I then distributed over 500 copies of the book —which I wrote in three weeks—without cost. .

Alice agreed to illustrate two more Nonnie books after *Nonnie/Quarantine*. I was thrilled.

Number 11, *Nonnie Talks about Relationships* took longer to write than any other book; I was diagnosed with my second breast cancer in the month I wrote the storyboard, and discovered as a patient what I knew as a nurse—pain does rob a person of energy.

Nonnie Talks about Mental Health was an obvious choice for #12 and my last book in the series. Mental health, stress, and the challenges our children and young people face permeate all the books in The Nonnie Series™. It was logical to end with it.

One day I hope to compile the hundreds of comments I've received from the Focus Groups I've held ever since *Nonnie Talks about Race*. Children and young people are wise to what is happening around them. Avoiding discussion about tough life topics can damage a young person and build walls between them and the trusted adults they need in their lives.

I wrote a book for adults to empower connection. *Sex Ed is in Session: An Adult Guide to Connecting with Young People about Life's Tough Topics*, was launched a week after our state locked down due to COVID; I then created a study guide to accompany it. Like all the books in The Nonnie Series™, it is available on Amazon, on my website, and at One Idea Press. https://www.oneideapress.com/product-page/sex-ed-is-in-session

Appendix 5: The Yellow Ribbon Campaign

Who is Yellow Ribbon

We are members of communities across this country/world who are empowering people (of all ages) to raise awareness about and to prevent youth/teen suicide. We coordinate appropriate education, training and collaboration with local and national resources, working directly with youth, many becoming Ambassadors, Trainers and Advisors.

Mission Statement

The Light for Life Foundation Int'l/Yellow Ribbon Suicide Prevention Program® is dedicated to preventing suicide and attempts by Making Suicide Prevention Accessible to Everyone and Removing Barriers to Help.

How It All Began

The program began in 1994 in response to heartfelt pleas from teens and adults after the death of a friend and loved one, Mike Emme (17). Words said by his family - "please don't do this, please talk to someone" were put on bright yellow paper along with phone numbers / who to call to get help. Teens pinned yellow ribbons on 500 slips of those yellow papers for his services and at the end, all were gone. Teens began to mail them 'everywhere' to friends and loved ones. Within three weeks came word of a girl who got help when she gave her yellow message* she had received in the mail to her teacher and received help. **The Ripple Effect had begun** - a bright yellow bridge that connects those in need to those who help.

~ The messages (yellow slips of paper) became the hallmark of the program – the Ask 4 Help!® Card.

Why Yellow?

Yellow became the symbol of the program when the teens began bringing us tons of yellow flowers and started tying yellow ribbons in their hair, pinning them on their clothes/hats on the day Mike died, in memory of Mike and his cherished yellow 1968 Ford Mustang. He helped so many people with that car.

Read the full story at www.yellowribbon.org *Our Story: Legacy of the Yellow Mustang*.

You can also read how it all started in Chicken Soup for the Soul: Third Serving (1997) and Chicken Soup for the Teenage Soul (2000).

THE RIPPLE EFFECT... what came next, see OUR WORK page.

To ask for some Ask4Help!® Cards: visit, call or email: www.yellowribbon.org

– 303-429-3530 - ask4help@yellowribbon.org

Author's Note: Thank you to Dale and Darlene Emme for their support.

Appendix 6: Centered Breathing

The APA (American Psychological Association) defines centering as:

A technique whose aim is to increase and focus attention and energy, to provide relief from stress and anxiety, or both. Various practices (e.g., meditation, yoga) emphasize centering as a way of focusing attention on the process of breathing in order to slow it down or regularize it. Sometimes this state of concentration is an end in itself. In other instances, at the point of concentration, negative thoughts and emotions are released and positive thoughts and emotions are encouraged. In sport psychology, the technique is used by athletes to assist them in achieving an ideal performance state.

In *Nonnie Talks about Mental Health* and other books in The Nonnie Series™, Dr. Mary Jo uses Nonnie to introduce the concept of centered breathing to Tamika, Alex, and their friends. In real life, she has taught children and young people to ease stress for decades.

Please remember there is no one way to center breathing. Each person is unique and able to find their own way to ease tension.

Dr. Mary Jo teaches centered breathing in three steps:
1. **Noticing breathing**
2. **Finding your center**
3. **Redirecting your energy**

A key to centered breathing is finding your center.

Most people take breaths without paying attention to them.
Be purposeful with your breathing.
As you inhale, notice the air enter your lungs as you take it in.
As you exhale, notice the air leave.
It may help to count slowly as you inhale and exhale.
Some people like to count to six or seven.
As you inhale, you may want to think, "I am breathing in."
As you exhale, you may want to think, "I am breathing out."

You may add to your thoughts as you notice your breathing.
You may think, "I am breathing in and I am okay."
You may think, "I am breathing out and I am at peace.'

Finding you center may mean you add mantras or affirmations, like:
"As I breathe in, I know all will be well."
"As I breathe out, I accept my feelings."

Finally, redirecting our energy means we reframe it from anger to peace, seeking joy.

Appendix 7: Substance Abuse/Addiction

The topic of substance abuse and addiction is linked closely with mental health.

Many people have a dual diagnosis of addiction and a DSM diagnosis.

Focus groups with children and young people initiated conversation about addiction in their lives, typically when adults they cared about dealt with substance abuse.

Nonnie Talks about Mental Health covers a great deal. Adding a detailed look at addiction was deemed overwhelming by the parents in our focus groups.

Here are some resources.

- **Addiction Center** offers online resources here: https://www.addictioncenter.com/community-resources/
- **The National Institute on Drug Abuse (NIDA)** resources are here: https://www.drugabuse.gov/publications/principles-drug-addiction-treatment-research-based-guide-third-edition/resources
- **NIDA** resources for teens can be found here: https://teens.drugabuse.gov/
- **The Partnership for Drug Free Kids** offers support here: https://drugfree.org/
- **The Society for Adolescent Health and Medicine** offers resources for young people here: https://www.adolescenthealth.org/Resources/Clinical-Care-Resources/Substance-Use/Substance-Use-Resources-For-Adolesc.aspx https://www.adolescenthealth.org/SAHM_Main/media/Clinical-Care-Resources/Substance-Use-one-pager-for-Adolescents_jhedt-FINAL.pdf
- **Substance Abuse and Mental Health Services Administration (SAMASA)** from the federal government offers support here: https://www.samhsa.gov/find-help/national-helpline

Appendix 8: A Parent's Wisdom

These ideas for coping strategies come from a dear friend, a professional with mental health experience, and a "mother whose been there."

Try to:

1. Keep to a schedule - it may help to go to bed and wake up at the same times.
2. Set a goal or two for each day and write them down, even if the goal is just to take a shower, wash hair, or brush teeth.
3. Put on clean clothes - even PJs.
4. Find something you like to do that brings some comfort- take a walk, listen to music, watch a favorite movie or tv show, garden…this should be personal and may vary from day to day.
5. Exercise may help ease stress.
6. Meditate, pray, keep a journal.
7. Talk to someone who listens- reach out to someone you trust.
8. Seek professional help when you need it; be strong and try to ignore the possible stigma of seeking help.
9. Take one day at a time.
10. Realize you can't control everything in life - most of life is not in our control - control what you can - let go what you can't. The hard part is knowing the difference. Think of The Serenity Prayer - *God, grant me the serenity to accept the things I cannot change, courage to change the things I can, and wisdom to know the difference.* (Sifton, 2003)
11. Not listen to news 24/7.
12. Limit social media before it becomes overwhelming.

Author's note: I would add one more tip…. Hold space (as Nonnie teaches Tamika and Alex) with others in need and be open to people holding space with you. The gift of another's presence is sacred.

Thank you to Deborah Calvarese Mahoney, Chuckie Mahoney Memorial Foundation

Sifton, Elisabeth. (2003). *The serenity prayer: Faith and politics in times of peace and war.* New York: Norton, 2003.

Glossary

Acceptance: From Thomas Gordan: Acceptance is like the fertile soil that permits a tiny seed to develop into the lovely flower it is capable of becoming. The soil only *enables* the seed to become the flower. It *releases* the capacity of the seed to grow, but the capacity is entirely within the seed. As with the seed, a child contains entirely within his organism the capacity to develop. Acceptance is like the soil – it merely enables the child to actualize his potential." *Thomas Gordon, P.E.T. Parent Effectiveness Training, 1970, p. 31*

Abuelito: Tamika's pet name for her grandpa.

Addiction; Addicted: An addiction is an urge to do something that is hard to control or stop. If people use cigarettes, alcohol, or drugs like marijuana (weed), cocaine, and heroin, they could become addicted to them.

Adopted: Legally made the child of adults who are not the child's biological parents (born to them). The adoptive parents raise the child.

Analogies: A comparison between two things. In Nonnie books, an analogy is often used to aid education.

Apprehensive: Fearful that something bad or unpleasant may happen.

Anxious: Feeling worry, unease, or nervousness.

Assesses: In counseling, when a counselor meets with a possible client to discover what the person needs to feel better. Dr. Rueben met with Alex to assess his depression.

Bipolar Disorder: A mental health condition that causes extreme mood swings that include emotional highs (mania or hypomania) and lows (depression). When you become depressed, you may feel sad or hopeless and lose interest or pleasure in most activities.

Blood Counts: Taking a sample of blood to assess a person's health. When Nonnie received chemotherapy, her white blood cell count was low, meaning she was susceptible to infection.

Body Language: The facial expressions and movements others can notice to figure out what people say without words.

Breast Cancer: A disease in which the cells of the breast grow out of control.

Glossary

Callout: Bring up a topic, often something difficult to talk about.

Centered Breathing: Please see Appendix 5 on page 81.

Challenges: An event or situation that are complicated or difficult and require an effort to get through.

Chemo: Chemotherapy: A drug treatment that uses powerful chemicals to kill fast-growing cells in your body. It is most often used to treat cancer. Chemo is a short way to say chemotherapy.

Chemo Caps: Coverings for the head after hair loss from chemo.

Clinically Depressed: A serious mental illness that negatively affects how a person thinks, feels and acts.

Common: Happening often to a large number of people.

Confidentiality: Keeping things shared in a counseling relationship a secret. Teens at the Teen Center know their words will be kept secret, unless they are a harm to themselves or to another. In that case, Nonnie tells them before she gets help.

Consistent: Acting the same way over time.

Counseling; Counselor: In this book, the means one person uses to guide another resolve personal, social or psychological problems through purposeful conversations. A counselor is a professional trained in counseling techniques.

Courage: The strength to do something frightening.

Crisis: When someone is "not in crisis" a person is not a danger to self or others.

Cutting: A common way to say self-harm among teens.

Depression: A common mental illness causing feelings of sadness and loss of interest in activities. Depression is treatable.

Diagnosed: When a person is given a diagnosis (when an illness or other problem is identified).

Disclose: Reveal, share. Typically used in case of abuse or another topic difficult to share or discuss.

Glossary

Disease: Something that makes a person unwell. World Health Organization's defines health is "a state of complete physical, mental and social well-being, not merely the absence of disease or infirmity" which makes the definition of disease broad and complicated.

DSM (Diagnostic and Statistical Manual of Mental Disorders): The handbook used by mental health professionals containing symptoms and descriptions for diagnosis.

Elephant in the Room: A topic people know is there, but ignored, such as death.

Emotions: Feelings like joy, sadness, anger…feelings are part of being human.

Empathy: The act of understanding, being aware of, being sensitive to, and vicariously experiencing the feelings, thoughts, and experience of another.

Enables: in this book, helps a person to grow.

Encourage: To inspire with courage, spirit and hope.

Energetic: Full of energy.

Fiancé: A person with whom one is engaged to be married. LeBron has a fiancé.

Foster Care: A temporary service for children who cannot live with their families. Also called out-of-home care.

Graphic: In this book, refers to pictures of private body parts sent via social media or texting.

Heroin: A highly addictive analgesic drug derived from morphine, often used illegally as a narcotic producing euphoria (extreme emotional highs).

Holding Space: The art of providing support without judgement, often in silence, without giving advice. Being there.

Inadequacy: Unable to deal with a situation in life.

Internship: A professional leaning experience that requires meaningful, practical work in a student's area of interest.

Glossary

Invisible: Not seen. If a person says they 'feel invisible' they often mean they feel ignored or unseen. Nonnie believes no one should be made to feel invisible.

Lockdown: In this book, lockdown refers to the physical isolation necessary during a pandemic. A lockdown may also occur in mass shooting drills, as in a school, or during an actual terrorist event. Please see *Nonnie Talks about Trauma*.

Medicine: In this book, drugs given to ease symptoms of mental illness.

Mental Health Problem: In contrast to a physical health problem, a mental illness.

Moody: Moving from one type of mood to another—happy to sad or angry. Mood swings.

National Junior Honor Society: The National Junior Honor Society (NJHS) elevates a school's commitment to the values of scholarship, service, leadership, character, and citizenship. These five pillars have been associated with membership in the organization since its inception in 1929.

Neglect: Failure to care for someone or something properly.

Nervous: Tending to be anxious, easily alarmed.

Nutrients: A substance that provides nourishment necessary to maintain life.

Obsessed: Fixated; unable to think of anything else.

One Day at a Time: A philosophy of living each day well and living in the present.

Pandemic: A disease happening over an entire country or the entire world.

Partner: In this context, a person with whom one is connected romantically or sexually. May also mean a person with whom one does business.

Pediatric Oncology: An area of expertise focused on the care of children with cancer. The real Nonnie worked in pediatric oncology as a young nurse.

Peer Educators: Young people trained to teach their peers (others of their own age or ability).

Peer Pressure: The feeling of being forced to do something to be accepted by peers.

Glossary

Peers: People the same age or similar abilities/backgrounds, etc.

Perfection: Being free of faults or defects. Flawless. No one is perfect.

Persistent: Continuing over a long period.

Perspective: How one sees things. Point of view.

Physical Problem: A problem dealing with the body's health, not the mind.

Psychologist: An expert or specialist in psychology.

Psychotherapy: Treatment of mental illness by psychological not medical means.

PTSD (Post Traumatic Stress Disorder): According to the American Psychiatric Association (APA): A psychiatric disorder that may occur in people who have experienced or witnessed a traumatic event such as a natural disaster, a serious accident, a terrorist act, war/combat, or rape or who have been threatened with death, sexual violence or serious injury. The APA is the leading scientific and professional organization representing psychology in the United States,

Puberty: Physical and emotional changes associated with growing from child to adult.

Pulling Away from Others: In this book, a red flag for depression; withdrawing from life's activities and connections.

Quarantine: Impose isolation.

Reassure: Say something to remove or ease doubts or fear.

Red Flags: In this book, signs of depression.

Research: Looking at a topic and examining it through study.

Respect: A polite and positive way of looking at someone and treating them. Respect means a person accepts others, even if they are different. It involves treating others with dignity. Respect can be learned.

Responsibilities: Having a duty to do something.

Glossary

Right to Speak or Pass: At the Teen Center, young people know their voices will be heard and respected. They also have the right to "pass", or not speak. These rights are part of the Teen Center guidelines.

Self-Harm: According to NAMH (National Alliance for Mental Health): Self-harm or self-injury means hurting yourself on purpose. One common method is cutting with a sharp object, but any time someone deliberately hurts themselves is classified as self-harm. For example, some people feel an impulse to pull out hair.

Self-Medicate: Easing stress or depression by using drugs/alcohol.

Side Effect; Something that happens as a result of taking a drug. In this book, a side effect of Nonnie's chemo is losing her hair.

Self-Worth: The opinion a person holds of self; the value a person places on self. Dr. Mary Jo (Nonnie) believes each person is a person of worth.

Soil: The upper layer of earth where plants grow.

Stigma: When a person is seen negatively because of mental illness; when counseling is looked down upon and judged.

Substance Abuse:

Suicide/Suicidal: Taking one's own life; the feeling/planning to take one's own life. Suicide is a permanent solution to a temporary problem.

Systemic Racism: A form of racism that is imbedded as normal practice in a society or an organization.

Therapy: Treatment for mental illness. In this book, synonymous with counseling.

Topic: A subject for conversation or discussion.

Trauma: A deeply disturbing or troubling experience.

Trusted Adults: Grown ups who mentor and support young people.

Unconscious: A state which occurs when the ability to maintain an awareness of self and environment is lost.

Unique: One of a kind. Each person is unique.

Glossary

Unwanted Touch: Any sexual contact done without consent. In this book, synonymous with rape or sexual abuse.

Vaccine: A substance used to stimulate the production of antibodies and provide immunity against one or several diseases.

Virtually: Not in person, as in online or via a phone or tablet.

Visible: Seen. Nonnie believes no one should be invisible.

Why (of her behavior): In trauma-informed care, a clinician seeks to understand the motivation or past history that causes people to act as they do.

Wigs: Coverings of hair worn on the head.

Worry: Give into anxiety; allow one's mind to focus on difficulty.

Worthy: When a person is seen as praiseworthy, having value. Worthiness refers to the feeling or belief of feeling worthy.

Endorsements

Consulting Authors

The Nonnie series has been such an inspiration to so many young people. I am honored to be able to offer a bit of my insight to this installment. Normalizing seeking help for mental and emotional issues is of the utmost importance to me. That's why I wanted to be involved with this book.

Dr. Rueben Brock

Among those of us who have devoted our lives toward working with young people, Mary Jo Podgurski is an icon. Her brain, her heart, and her inexhaustible energy are legendary. Her "*Nonnie*" series covers critical concerns of young people. I am flattered to be able to contribute toward helping normalize counseling in the service of enhancing mental health. This book addresses many of the challenges facing young people today.

Robert Selverstone, Ph.D.

Endorsements

Mary Jo, this is a lovely piece of work. I can feel your love and passion in its words. You explain these issues in such a caring, nonjudgmental way. Thank you for sharing! ♡

Karen Bennett
Washington Community Behavioral Health Advocate and Volunteer

Dr. Podgurski has always had the right words, and this book is nothing different. Mental health is probably one of the hardest topics to discuss, especially with young people, but, once again, it's made easy by Dr. Mary Jo. I'm forever thankful for the kind words and complex situations that are made as simple as possible.

LaShauna Carruthers, 18

Nonnie Talks about Mental Health is so very much needed in this world today, and your style and approach are so inviting and yet deeply involved for difficult topics. We find people are very good at one thing when dealing with kids and are afraid to ask them how we can help with whatever is happening to them or around them. You clearly give youth the tools they need for whatever the issue that confronts them. You clearly know youth, care about them and are more than willing to share the answers they seek, but also the process needed to help and thrive.

Dale and Darlene Emme
Co-founders, Yellow Ribbon Suicide Prevention Program® .

Endorsements

Nonnie Talks about Mental Health is an essential addition to Dr. Podgurski's Nonnie Series. Seeing signs of mental health disturbances, of emotional distress, is not uncommon for young people. They see it in their peers, they see it in the adults around them. Adults are often unsure about what they are seeing, and even more uncertain about what to do in response, and this is even more confusing and often frightening for youth. This book doesn't pretend to have all the answers; this book shows how to open the doors to awareness, insight, compassion, and action.

One doesn't need to have read the other books to benefit from this one, but if you have, do know that Dr. P -- a Nonnie for real!! -- weaves together the characters and events of all her Nonnie books, to offer us one that can so genuinely and simply help young people understand mental health conditions, and help the adults who care for them guide that understanding.

I endorse this book not just as a professional, but as a mother and grandmother.

Thank you again, Dr. P!!

Joan Garrity
Educator and Trainer

Mary Jo Podgurski has never been a stranger to tough conversations, and her latest work is no exception to this rule! *Ms. Nonnie Talks About Mental Health* provides a straight-forward yet sensitive lens into a subject that matters not only in the general sense, but to the scores and scores of particular young people facing unprecedented challenges in this area. At a time when many adults find themselves struggling with how to effectively talk about mental health with young people (or even validate the real-time issues they face), this newest addition to the *Nonnie* series provides both valuable tools and exercises for young people, and concrete examples for the askable adults in their lives for how to keep the conversation going long after this story ends. Brava, Mary Jo; would highly recommend!

Tracie Q. Gilbert, PhD
Founder, ThembiAnaiya.com
Culturally-Sensitive education for multicultural and under-resourced communities.

The story was great, it flowed really nicely. I enjoyed it a LOT, and the little bit of romance at the end is the cherry on top! Thank you for letting me review it. The book asks questions, and you can talk to someone about things that matter, which will definitely make them feel better.

Shea Hatfield, 13

Endorsements

What a hard topic to delve into with adolescents: mental health, depression, anxiety and sadness. All approached with the ease that only Nonnie can accomplish. This book is timely because many of our children are experiencing so many of these issues. Covid has upset the apple cart of development and many will be arrested in 2020 for years to come. Nonnie addresses these mental health issues in a comprehensive, easy to understand manner for children of all ages. Nonnie centers the experiences of our youth and calms their anxiety with easy to understand responses. Like all of her other books, Nonnie listens to adolescents. I am sad that this the last installation of Nonnie. I am sure that we will see Nonnie again. I highly recommend this work, as it calms fears, addresses reality, and speaks the language of our youth.

Monique S Howard, EdD, MPH
Executive Director, WOAR- Philadelphia Center Against Sexual Violence

In this 12th edition of the Nonnie series, Mary Jo compassionately and sensitively speaks to the topic of mental health and suicide for young readers and their families. The language employed and the approach to the topic shows a trauma-informed approach and aims to reduce stigma around mental health treatment and diagnosis. Many readers and their families will also relate to the timely situations and concerns incorporated into the book, making it a relevant and educational piece of literature for readers young and old.

Joseph Mahoney, LSW
Director of Mental/Behavioral Health and Social Work Services-Intermediate Unit 1

Nonnie talks about mental health breaks down the complexities of real world problems by using relatable situations young adults will find themselves in. The ability to use examples of problems in the book to help young adults guide themselves through mental health situations allows trusted adults to know their young people are set up for success. A great addition to the already amazing Nonnie talks series of books.

Rodney Maze RN
Sergeant, US Army Infantry, Operation Iraqi freedom 2008-2009.
Registered Nurse.

Nonnie Talks about Mental Health is an engaging, easy to read book full of factual information for teens, their parents and those who want to learn about mental illness and substance use in teens. Definitions and activities to reinforce the main themes are straightforward and applicable.

Everyone should have a Nonnie in their life.

Joni Schwager, LSW,
Executive Director, Staunton Farm Foundation

Endorsements

Reading *Nonnie Talks about Mental Health* made me smile because Nonnie has already talked about mental health in the eleven books that preceded this one. Whether Nonnie is talking about death, disability, gender, race, religion, sex, or any other topic, every *Nonnie* book is an exercise in reducing shame and stigma, while role modeling respect and compassion for the young learners and the adults who care about them.

Bill Taverner
Chief Editor, *American Journal of Sexuality Education*

Nonnie Series™ Focus Groups: Since the 2nd book in The Nonnie Series™, Focus Groups for children in grades 3—4, 5-6 and 7-8 are held prior to publication.

The comments and suggestions from these young people are often poignant and wise. Here are a few from the groups for *Nonnie Talks About Mental Health*.

3rd and 4th graders:
I like the way Tamika and Alex help each other. I learned it's good to tell a trusted adult if you feel sad like Alex.

3rd grader

I felt lost when our school shut down, too. It helped to read about Alex and the way he felt just like I did.

4th grader

5th and 6th graders:
My dad was depressed and had to go to a hospital to get better. He sees a doctor every week. He's a lot better now.

5th grader

Last year my big sister did the same thing as LeBron's friend Josh in the book. I'm glad there were people to help her. This book helped me see she can get better.

6th grader

7th and 8th graders:
I have social anxiety and ADHD. Sometimes I am depressed. The book made me feel like I'm not alone.

7th grader

My best friend's older brother took his own life three years ago. He was 17. I will never ever forget the funeral. You ask me if children are too young for this topic. I say absolutely not. I was certainly affected by this death. Thank you for writing this book.

8th grader

Dr. Mary Jo Podgurski is the founder and director of The Washington Health System Teen Outreach and the Academy for Adolescent Health in Washington, Pa.

She is a nurse, a counselor, a parent, a trainer and speaker, and an educator who is dedicated to serving young people. The Outreach has reached over 250,000 young people since 1988. Check out www.healthyteens.com for information on the Academy and its programs.

Dr. Mary Jo is certified as a childbirth educator through Lamaze International, as a sexuality educator and a sexuality counselor through AASECT (American Association for Sexuality Educators, Counselors and Therapists.

She is an authorized facilitator for the Darkness to Light abuse prevention program and a certified trainer for the Olweus Bullying Prevention Program. Dr. Mary Jo is the author of the *Ask Mary Jo* weekly column in the *Observer-Reporter* newspaper and answers 6—10 questions from young people daily.

he wrote Nonnie Talks about Gender in 2014 as a labor of love and the Nonnie Series™ was birthed!

Most importantly, Dr. Mary Jo and her partner Rich are the parents of three wonderful adult children and are blessed to be grandparents. She is a Nonnie in Real Life!

Dr. Mary Jo believes ally is a verb.
She believes in social and racial justice.
She believes in young people.
She believes each person is a person of worth. Please pass it on.

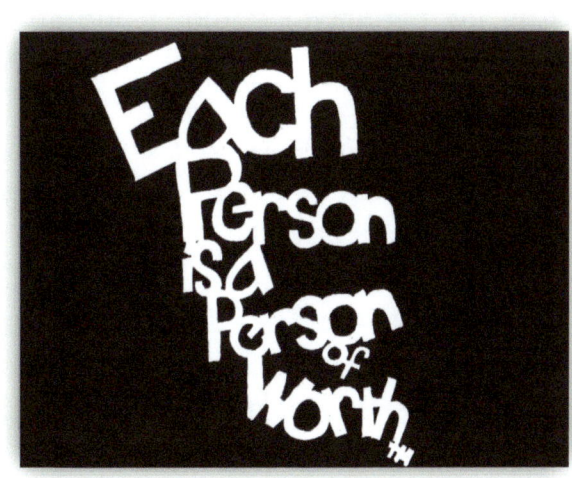

About the Nonnie Series

Writing *Nonnie Talks about Gender* in the summer of 2014 was a true labor of love. The idea of a "Nonnie Series" never entered my mind. The reactions to *Nonnie Talks about Gender* surprised and humbled me. I began to realize gender wasn't the only challenging topic in our world. Social media and 24-hour news have created information overload, where even elementary school children are inundated with potentially confusing and troubling subjects. How should adults open the door to these teachable moments?

As a young nurse I became a birth advocate; as a certified Lamaze childbirth educator I have continued my commitment to birthing women and families since the 1970s. In 1973, I began working with pediatric oncology at Memorial Sloan Kettering Cancer Center in New York City. My passion for birthing normally dovetailed with my growing commitment for death with dignity. I became a hospice nurse in the 1980s. Long before the "circle of life" became part of a popular film for children, I learned how vital birth and death are to the human experience...and how often both topics are avoided when talking with children. *Nonnie Talks about Pregnancy and Birth* and *Nonnie Talks about Death* followed.

As an ally and advocate for racial and social justice, I cannot ignore how much our culture needs to address racial equity. Then, as I was presenting my child abuse prevention program, *Inside Out, Your Body is Amazing Inside and Out and Belongs Only to YOU*, an eight-year-old child told me what #BlackLivesMatter meant to her. We talked, I listened. This little one's very real fear that her own life was less worthy than another's based on the color of her skin was my inspiration for *Nonnie Talks about Race*.

Nonnie Talks about Puberty was born because another child needed it. I began teaching growing up classes called "What's Up as You Grow Up" in 1984. Gender non-conforming children are often confused during puberty; I couldn't find an inclusive resource on growing up, so I wrote one. Empathy is a learned skill. I hope all children will benefit from the book.

As a sexologist, *Nonnie Talks about Sex…& More*, was a no-brainer for my next book. *Nonnie Talks about Trauma* was written as a direct result to young people's reactions to the Parkland shooting. I tried to offer a balanced approach. The Let's Talk program really happened in our community. *Nonnie Talks about Consent* and *Nonnie Talks about Disability* came from the needs of children and young people today. *Nonnie Talks about Quarantine,* was written in 3 weeks in March, 2020, and distributed without cost to over 500 parents/teachers. *Nonnie Talks about Relationships,* and *Nonnie Talks about Mental Health* complete the series.

Please connect with me at podmj@healthyteens.com with feedback and thoughts.

**Did you enjoy
Nonnie Talks about Mental Health?
Hope to encourage empathy with**
Nonnie Talks about Disability?
**Want to prepare children for
relationships by
teaching with** Nonnie Talks about Consent
and Nonnie Talks about Relationships?
Need guidance for a pandemic with
Nonnie Talks about Quarantine?
See the need for
Nonnie Talks about Trauma?
Want to use
Nonnie Talks about Sex…& More
to add to 'the talk' with a young person?
Can your family use
Nonnie Talks about Death?
Interested in Nonnie Talks about Puberty?
Curious about Nonnie Talks about Race?
Intrigued by
Nonnie Talks about Pregnancy and Birth?
Wonder about Nonnie Talks about Gender?
**Entranced by the concept of the
Nonnie Series™?**

Dr. Mary Jo has dedicated her
life to empowering young people.
She strives to model her motto of
"Each Person is a Person of Worth"
through education, writing, and trainings.
She is available for workshops and consultation.
She is also the author of 38 books.
You can find her books, including the Nonnie Series™,
at Amazon or on her website, drmaryjopodgurski.com
You can reach her at:

Email: podmj@healthyteens.com
http://www.healthyteens.com/
Toll free #: 1 (888) 301-2311
Twitter DrMaryJoPod

www.ingramcontent.com/pod-product-compliance
Lightning Source LLC
Chambersburg PA
CBHW041701160426
43191CB00003B/51